THE
NINE VALUES
THAT SHAPED
GREAT
BRITAIN

WHY 'NICE' WON'T SAVE US

GAVIN P. FRASER

Edited by Tim Hammerton

Book design by Andy Thesen DTP

Cover design by Sourav Bhattacharyya

ISBN paperback: 978-1-0369-6707-9

To those who sacrificed and struggled for freedom.
And to those whom this book may inspire.

Preface

Something has gone terribly wrong in Britain. No one quite dares say what it is, so the void gets filled with half-baked clichés. If asked what British values are, the average politician will mumble "tolerance", "fairness", and "compassion" as if those weren't shared by every halfway civilised country on earth. The comedians and columnists add their own stock-in-trade: bad teeth, bad plumbing, worse food. And the critics, particularly the self-loathing ones, reach for the nuclear option: "colonialists", "racists", and "slavers".

This is what passes for the story of Britain today—a country reduced to punchlines and indictments, stripped of the facts of its history. And what has Britain's political class done to counter this? Precious little. Years of uniparty mush.

And yet, something stirs. Drive through towns and villages and you'll notice more St George's flags and Union Jacks fluttering from windows and pub roofs. Britons sense they are being told to be ashamed of who they are, and their instinct is to push back—quietly, but firmly, like the eerie calm before the storm. The tragedy is that, even now, few dare to name Britain's values, trace where they came from, or explain why they matter. Perhaps the British themselves are too cowed, too weary of being called, racists, or colonial nostalgists, to make the case aloud.

But the case must be made. Britain did not move from tribal squabbles and despotic kingships to constitutional monarchy and parliamentary liberty, by accident. It did not stumble blindly from mud huts to Magna Carta. It forged values along the way—rough-hewn at first but polished over centuries—values that explain why this small island has punched so far above its weight. They explain how Britain became the nation that advanced liberty more than any other, and why its civic code remains the template for the world's most successful societies.

I came to Britain at the age of thirty-three, an immigrant from South Africa, and I have always felt incredibly privileged to live here. Even after decades, I still have a sense of wonder every time I pass Buckingham Palace.

I have never lost that gratitude. But I have also seen, with growing dismay, how Britain has allowed itself to be caricatured, diminished, and misunderstood. And so, I write this book not to point fingers, but to help. To help Britons regain their self-confidence, and to help non-Britons—whether immigrants or residents—understand what it takes to thrive here.

And I will try to do it in British style: with humility, with wry humour, and with facts. Because Britain is too important to the world to be left voiceless, too exceptional to be dismissed, and too precious to be forgotten.

In 1995, I stood in the crowd in Hyde Park at the fiftieth anniversary of the end of the Second World War in Europe and heard Vera Lynn sing. I grew up listening to one of the few records my parents had, her *Hits of the Blitz*. The cover was her sitting smiling on the rubble of a building destroyed by Nazi Germany. The songs of a nation's endurance, of sacrifice and hope, carried across the generations. I was smiling with tears streaming down my face. It moved me profoundly.

My grandparents were all from Britain—three from Scotland, one from England—so the sense of belonging was always there. My English gran watched the late Queen crown her twenty-year-old son, Charles, as Prince of Wales not once, not twice, but more than twenty times—in a special mid-afternoon cinema showing in downtown Cape Town. She lived an hour away by train, often found herself the only person in the cinema, and cried every single time as though it were the first. The year was 1969.

Growing up in an ex-colony, Britain was our beacon. Everything arrived in South Africa slowly by mail ship: spare parts for the lathe on which I made a chess set, the eagerly awaited children's annuals as Christmas presents for myself and my siblings. Britain, though distant, was vivid in my imagination. For me, Britain was jigsaw puzzles of Cotswold villages, Enid Blyton's Famous Five and Secret Seven, the mysteries of Agatha Christie, the music of Elgar. As a stamp collector, I collected every stamp from every country which had an image of Charles and Diana at the time of their marriage. True confession.

When I arrived in 1991, Britain seemed to me to be booming with confidence. But as time passed, particularly after the first Blair years, Britain seemed increasingly unhappy with itself. A cultural war was under way. History was being rewritten. A new narrative was being crafted. Nothing Britain had achieved was admired; the nation that had contributed so much to civilisation was increasingly treated as an embarrassment or worse.

Facts no longer mattered. Selective outrage, double standards and hypocrisy replaced truth. The BBC, once the voice of national confidence, appeared increasingly biased against the very country it represented. Britain was being taught to despise itself. It seemed that when people spoke of "British values" they came up with little beyond those mentioned already, as well as "being nice" and "queueing". It seemed ridiculous, a parody of a nation's character and not the country I thought I understood.

This book argues that British values are not a vague mishmash of such weak tea as "being nice" or "tolerance" or "queueing". They are specific, hard-won, and unique. They grew out of centuries of enormous struggle, reform, and persistence. They have contributed disproportionately to humankind. And they deserve to be understood, honoured, and, above all, defended.

Even though Britain's culture was familiar to me through books, music, and family, I still struggled at first to make sense of Britons in practice. And I made mistakes—some small, some mortifying.

The Barbour Incident

When I received my first salary cheque in Britain, I knew exactly what I wanted to buy. A Barbour jacket. Not just any jacket, but *the* jacket—a waxed green badge of Britishness, sturdy and practical yet quietly stylish. I bought mine from Harrods, no less, and walked out wearing it feeling that I was finally woven into the very fabric of Britain.

On Monday morning I wore it proudly to the office. We worked in a Georgian building just off Berkeley Square. Pat, our formidable office manager, an ex-military veteran with a cut-glass accent, took one look and gasped.

"Oh no, Gavin, you *cannot* wear that!"

Before I knew it, she had prised it off my shoulders and flung it on the floor at the entrance.

"Leave it here until everyone arrives," Pat declared, eyes flashing. "I want them to walk all over it." I stood frozen, concerned that the weatherproof wax coating would be damaged.

Humiliation burned. I watched as colleagues trod on my precious Harrods purchase.

Later that day, Pat whisked the jacket off to an expensive dry cleaner, and by evening it was back in my hands, looking miraculously … better. The shine was gone. The jacket looked comfortably worn, as if it had been in the family for generations.

When I slipped it on, I suddenly understood. Around me, my colleagues were wearing their own Barbours over expensive suits, every one of them scuffed, faded, patched, softened by years of use. Their jackets looked like heirlooms, passed from father to son, mother to daughter. My shiny new purchase had screamed "outsider". Pat had turned it into an insider's garment in a single day.

That was Britain. Quality, understated. A reverence for the old, the tried, the tested—and a deep suspicion of anything too obviously new. I had thought I was buying my way into Britain. What I really needed was to understand it.

The Barbour incident was a small blip and amusing to look back on. But there were other things. Had a book like this existed when I arrived, it would have saved me time, embarrassment, and confusion. It would have explained why certain things mattered to the British when they seemed trivial to outsiders, and how to avoid the faux pas that can make an immigrant feel more alien than they really are.

I am writing this book as a reminder to the Britons of their values and what they have achieved, and a guide for those who come to Britain and genuinely wish to belong, not as an exercise in nostalgia, prejudice, or politics.

What is "Britain"?

I use *Britain* as shorthand for the United Kingdom in its various historical forms—recognising that borders have shifted, unions have been forged and sometimes broken, and the story is, like the weather here, rarely straightforward.

In short: when I say *Britain*, think of the evolving union of these islands that produced the values and institutions I am exploring here. If the terminology makes you frown—welcome to the club. Britain itself has never been entirely sure what to call itself either.

"British Values" or "UK Values"

All through this book I use the phrase *British values*. Some will ask why not *UK values*, since the political entity is the United Kingdom. It is a fair question.

The truth is that *British values* carries a resonance that *UK values* does not. *UK values* sounds like something from a government white paper, stripped of music and memory. *British values*, by contrast, summon the bells, the hedgerows, the market square and cricket pitches, the scepticism and the humour. It has warmth, history, and cultural weight.

The fabric of what I call British values is woven from many strands: the stubbornness of the Scots, the lyricism of the Welsh, the industry of the English, the resilience of the Irish, the seafaring grit of the Cornish, and the legacy of those who invaded and stayed—Normans, Vikings, Saxons, and others besides. Over centuries, these threads fused into something distinct, recognisable, and enduring.

So, I use *British values* not to exclude, but to embrace. It is the broadest, richest name we have for the character of these islands. And if you doubt it, watch a railway platform at rush hour: Scots, Welsh, Irish, and English alike, all muttering at the late train, but still queuing together in perfect order.

Who are the "Non-Britons'

In this book, I use the term "non-Britons" for brevity. It is not meant as negative or exclusionary, and I apologise if it unintentionally causes offence. By it I mean "those outside the British story", people like myself living in the UK without having been steeped in its long inheritance of values over centuries. It is not a term of disparagement, nor of permanent exclusion. *Britain's values are not tied to bloodlines* but are a living inheritance, open to anyone willing to embrace them. The phrase simply distinguishes between those who have inherited and shaped British values across centuries and those who have not yet done so.

That includes multigeneration immigrants who may have embraced these values, others who live more by their ancestors' cultural codes, migrant workers, asylum seekers, students, long-term residents, tourists, and even spouses with foreign passports.

Who Characterised the Non-Britons' Alignment to British Values

In this book, I suggest categories of how non-Britons align with the nine values: those who've fitting in with grace, those still finding their footing and those struggling most to find common ground. Such classifications can be contentious, so I did not invent them alone. Instead, I drew on the "big data" capabilities of AI, which distils patterns across vast sources far faster—and with fewer blind spots— than I could have.

These categories are not judgments of worth but broad observations, which will all have exceptions. They aim to explain why some groups adapt easily to British Values while others struggle more. The purpose is constructive: to illuminate, not to condemn. Britain's own values demand such honest dialogue, even in an age when open debate too often feels threatened.

The Arc of the Book

Britain once lit the torch of liberty, fairness, and invention—and passed it around the world. But somewhere along the way, we set the torch down, forgot where we put it, and allowed others to tell us our story. This book argues that Britain's greatness was never accidental; it was driven principally by nine values, forged and tested in crisis, and embedded in everything from Parliament to puddings. Today, the unravelling of those values explains our national confusion. But if we can name them, defend them, and live by them again, Britain will not just muddle through—it will lead once more.

Chapter 1: The Great Unravelling: When a Nation Forgets What It Stands For introduces Britain's strange inability to name its own values, and shows how this silence has led to drift, discontent, and a people growing increasingly restless on both the political right, centre and left.

Chapter 2: Nine, Not "Nice': The Values that Shaped Great Britain reveals upfront a short description of the values—better in this case to know the score before watching the match, so every later chapter can be read with the values already in play.

Chapter 3: The Island That Changed Humanity: Britain's Astonishing Achievements reminds us how one damp island gave the world parliaments, common law, limited government, steam engines, Shakespeare, penicillin, and the Beatles—and wonders why Britain now blushes at its own triumphs.

Chapter 4: Forged in Fire and Rain: The Long Making of British Values explains how, with no manual for building a free society, Britain improvised through centuries of trial and error—and asks whether any other nation could have done it better.

Chapter 5: The Nine British Values in Detail: What They Are (and Definitely Are Not) finally does what Briton's seem reluctant to do—it sets out nine values in a little detail and defines what they are not.

Chapter 6: The Bells, the Market Square, the Cricket Pitch: How Values Shape the Sights and Sounds of Britain shows why bells, hedgerows, and market squares reveal more about Britain than any speech—and why life feels foreign the moment these quiet signals disappear.

Chapter 7: Can You Join the Queue? How Non-Britons Adapt— or Don't explores the habits of those who adapt with courage and humour, those who are caught between different value systems, and those who seem to barge through, perhaps unintentionally, as if the market square were a hostile battlefield.

Chapter 8: How Outsiders Win Britain's Heart: From Nadiya's Bake-Off Smile to Mo Farah's Finish Line shows how bakers, runners, and newscasters become national treasures—and why affection vanishes the moment people refuse to join in.

Chapter 9: At War with Ourselves: Britain Without Its Values reveals the massive cost of neglecting old instincts—potholes unfilled, freedoms curtailed, crime unpunished, non-crimes investigated— and asks whether today's mess is more about leaders for decades unrelentingly sawing against the national grain.

Chapter 10: When Britain Remembers Who It Is: The Peculiar Island That Once Led the World—and Can Again makes the case that rediscovering what once worked is not nostalgia but necessity if Britain is going to play a leading role, as it has done before, in moving the world to a freer, more prosperous and fairer one.

So that's the plan. Ten chapters, nine values, and one slightly battered island trying to remember who it is. Because if we can name what made us strong, we can be strong again—not through slogans or flags, but through the quiet courage of living by our own hard-won rules.

Contents

Preface   v

1. **The Great Unravelling:** When a nation forgets what it
    stands for   1

2. **Nine, Not "Nice":** The Values that Shaped Great Britain   10

3. **The Island That Changed Humanity:** Britain's Astonishing
    Achievements   14

4. **Forged in Fire and Rain:** The Long Making of British
    Values   20

5. **The Nine British Values:** What They Are (and Definitely
    Are Not)   39

6. **The Bells, the Market Square, the Cricket Pitch:**
    How Values Shape the Sights and Sounds of Britain   50

7. **Can You Join the Queue?:** How Non-Britons
    Adapt—or Don't   57

8. **How Outsiders Win Britain's Heart:** From Nadiya's
    Bake-Off Smile to Mo Farah's Finish Line   72

9. **At War With Ourselves:** Britain Without Its Values   80

10. **When Britain Remembers Who It Is:** The Peculiar Island
    That Once Led the World—and Can Again   87

Epilogue: Play Your Part   95

Bibliography   99

About the Author   101

1 The Great Unravelling

When a nation forgets what it stands for

Nations fall in many ways—through invasion, famine, or tyranny. Britain's danger is quieter but no less deadly: it has forgotten what it stands for.

In the void, leaders are stacking new laws on foundations that are not our own—borrowed blueprints, alien frameworks, "global" scaffolding. And the result is inevitable. The further Britain drifts from its bedrock, the more the cracks widen. We see them already—in politics, in public trust, in the economy, in harassment of ordinary people and cover-ups for criminals, and in the market square. Unless Britain finds its footing again, the very ground beneath us will give way.

Finding British Values

I searched high and low for Britain's values—it turns out they're harder to find than the Loch Ness Monster.

Ask a Briton to define British values and you'll usually get silence, a cough, and at last something about "tolerance" or "being nice". Then someone mutters, "queueing". If this is our national creed, no wonder the country feels lost.

I looked up and contacted https://www.uk-values.org/research but found they were testing attitudes to various issues such as immigration, institutions, neighbourhoods, parenting, social trust and so on. Here's the difference: values are your DNA; attitudes are just your outfit for the day, and they can change rapidly.

Back in 2002, David Blunkett said "Britishness is defined not on ethnic and exclusive grounds but through shared values; our history of tolerance, openness and internationalism" (BrainyQuote, 2002). Tolerance, openness and internationalism aren't really values—they're more like good table manners on the global stage.

David Cameron had a better go in 2014:

> *The values I'm talking about—a belief in freedom, tolerance of others, accepting personal and social responsibility, respecting and upholding the rule of law—are the things we should try to live by every day.*
> (UK Government, 15 June 2014)

Cameron was on the right track, but padding the list with tolerance and law-abidingness is a bit like adding "don't run in corridors" to the Ten Commandments.

Governments have never been shy of making lists. Since 2011, our Department for Education (and Michael Gove, Education Secretary in July 2014 in *The Guardian*) has pushed schools to "actively promote" a neat little set called Fundamental British Values: "democracy, the rule of law, individual liberty, mutual respect, and tolerance". All sound familiar, all sound vaguely reassuring. But here's the catch: most of these are not values in the deep sense of the word. They are, at best, attributes of any half-decent democratic state. More scaffolding than stonework.

Douglas Murray, bestselling writer, cultural critic, and scourge of lazy platitudes, summarised the problem with stating British values now in a speech at the Oxford Union (31 January 2014) saying that the British have been reduced to saying things like "Britishness is about … being nice to people".

"Nice"! A word so bloodless it could be embroidered on a tea towel. A word fit for describing a Victoria sponge, not a nation that forged the modern world.

Niceness Can Be Weakness

Niceness is a splendid quality in a neighbour who feeds your cat or hands back your lost umbrella. But as the organising principle of a civilisation? It doesn't quite do the job. Nobody marched at Agincourt or stormed the beaches of Normandy shouting, "Be nice!"

Tolerance can become appeasement

Tolerance sounds noble, until you realise it can mean tolerating things that no sane society should. Do we "tolerate" burglars out of respect for their lifestyle choices? At that point, tolerance stops being a virtue and starts looking suspiciously like cowardice in a cardigan. Appeasement, wrapped up in polite packaging, is still appeasement.

Moral clarity gets blurred

If tolerance and niceness are treated as absolutes, you end up with moral uncertainty. To tolerate everything is to stand for nothing. To be "nice" to everyone is to betray those who deserve loyalty. A country that tries to live only by these two airy virtues can find itself shaking hands with tyrants while leaving its allies in the lurch—all because it was too polite to say "not on".

The British instinct is firmer

Britain's genius has never been saccharine slogans. Britons don't mind being decent, but they also know when to say "no". We didn't stand alone in 1940 by being "nice". We did it by being bloody-minded and stubborn. Against the battering rams of ideology, grievance mongering, or revisionist history, "niceness", "tolerance", and "queuing" won't hold the line.

Real values are lived habits, forged over centuries. They seep into how people wait their turn, argue, apologise, and laugh. By contrast, the official list feels like wallpaper—a cover-up after the plaster has already started to crumble. It is as though Whitehall hopes that if you slap "mutual respect" without mutual responsibilities onto a school poster, it will mend fractures caused by ignoring the values that already existed and worked. For the moment, let's see what happens when these values are forgotten.

Everyone seems to be increasingly unhappy. The right, the centre, the left, those non-Britons who have been here for generations, and those struggling to integrate.

The Right: "Bring Back the Backbone"

For the right, Britain's problem isn't a lack of compassion but a surplus of it, even "suicidal empathy". A nation that once built railways, defeated tyranny, and invented the concept of fair play now seems unsure whether it's allowed to be proud of any of it. The right looks around and sees a country that apologises before it speaks—a reflex of guilt taught by decades of one-sided cultural self-criticism against a utopian ideal. They believe institutions like the BBC, the civil service, and the universities have swapped merit for moral signalling, replacing standards with slogans. Immigration, once a managed flow of workers and families for Britain's benefit, now feels to them like a house without a door. The world's orphanage. And in Parliament, they see too much careerism and too little courage—politicians who will stand for any cause that trends on social media but none that might cost them votes. So they are all things to all people.

In their eyes, Britain's become a country that files risk assessments before planting its flag—and wonders why nobody salutes.

The Centre: "Where's the Manual?"

The centre views Britain not as broken, but badly organised—a nation that still has fine instincts but terrible paperwork. These are the people who don't want a culture war; they just want their trains to run, their bins collected, and their leaders to tell the truth without a footnote. The middle ground believes the real issue is managerial decay: institutions once admired for competence now wobble like badly assembled modular furniture. The NAtional Health Service (NHS) is loved but lumbering; the civil service is clever but paralysed by bureaucracy; and local councils seem able to ban plastic straws but not fill potholes. They long for leadership that is calm, decent, and practical—something closer to a national headteacher than a messianic influencer.

They suspect Britain doesn't need saving; it just needs rebooting—preferably without another committee on rebooting.

The Left: "Fair Shares, Finally"

For the left, Britain's ailment is inequality, and for some on the left, inequity—a country that talks of fair play but too often rigs the game. They see a gilded London skyline rising above food banks, hedge-fund bonuses announced the same week as school budget cuts, and public services stretched thinner than the paper of a Treasury report. To them, British values have been hijacked by those with the loudest microphones: fairness means little if the economic dice seem to remain loaded. They point to the rise of zero-hours contracts, stagnant wages, and unaffordable housing as evidence that the system protects the privileged, not the public. And they resent the moral amnesia of those who praise past greatness while ignoring present hardship.

Their dream is still the same: that the wealth of Britain—moral, cultural, and financial—should not trickle downward but be shared outward, past London, past privilege, past pretence.

Non-Britons Who've Made Britain Home

Many who came to Britain brought with them a remarkable adaptability. They saw in Britain a place that rewarded effort, humour, and contribution, and they met it on its own terms. These non-Britons tend to flourish because they understand the quiet British social contract: work hard, contribute more than you take out, mind your business, join the Parent Teachers Association, be honest about your mistakes and remember to laugh at yourself.

They've learned that to be accepted in Britain you don't need to demand to be made to feel welcome—just roll up your sleeves, get stuck in, contribute to everyone's well-being, and say "sorry" even when someone else bumps into you, just like the Britons do.

Non-Britons Still Finding Their Feet

For others the journey to belonging has been more complicated. They often arrive from societies where family and clan carry massively more weight than individual liberty, and where other ethnic groups in the country, or the state, is something to fear, not to trust. In Britain, the state is seen as incredibly generous and can easily be taken for granted, without realising that British fairness is a two-way street, not endless charity. Asylum seekers are seen as adults, not orphans to be forever supported.

Britain, with its habit of quiet understatement, can seem difficult to intuit, even bewildering. Integration doesn't fail because of malice but because the code is unspoken—a thousand little customs that only make sense after years of contact. But for many non-Britons too much contact with Britons may be ill-advised or feared. For some, there is an inherited caution towards assimilation, which for some is seen as surrender or capitulation. So, fitting in seems inadvisable. The result is that succeeding in Britain is far more difficult and seems hopeless. The perception is that the deck of cards may be stacked against them.

So What Now?

Britain's standing on global happiness has slipped visibly from 13th place in 2020 to 23rd place in 2025 in the World Happiness Report—its lowest rank in years.

Something in Britain is not just creaking anymore. It is groaning. Splintering. Promises reversed. Freedoms clipped. Council taxes hiked. A rising cry that streets are less safe, voices less free. The quiet muttering of a year ago has turned into a roar. Anger bubbles in pubs, in town halls, and online. Words like "civil war"—once unthinkable here—have been pushed into public view by some leaders, echoed by warfare academics, and magnified by protests and online platforms. Whether literal or metaphorical, it signals a deep anxiety about whether Britain can hold itself together.

When leaders post on social media, *criticisms* can receive more "likes" than the post. The mood is reaching fever pitch. Every week loads another straw on the camel's back. What felt like drift a year ago now feels like a slide. Not steady but accelerating. Exponentially worse, month by month.

This is Britain's unravelling: a country that once clothed the world in fairness now pulls at the loose threads of its own fabric. The weave is fraying, seams splitting. Where the flag once flew with confidence, its colours now look faded, overshadowed by bolder banners held higher in the public square. It is even seen by some as a racist symbol. What unravels is not only cloth but meaning—the very sense of what Britain stands for. The tragedy is not just the chaos, but the cause: a nation tugging apart the very fabric that gave it strength.

Take politics. U-turns have become the national sport. The mandated majority threshold of the country voted for Brexit but got Brexit with a thousand asterisks. Britain voted to "take back control" of immigration, yet the numbers soared. Politicians promised cuts; the floodgates opened wider. Refugee hotels sprang up in coastal towns faster than fish and chip shops in the old days. Promises made, promises broken.

Look at the law. Citizens feel their rights shrinking. They feel that the European Court of Human Rights seems to guard the rights of anyone but them. Habeas corpus once meant you couldn't be banged up without cause. Now free speech itself feels on remand. A tweet can land you in more hot water than burglary. The burglar probably won't even be investigated.

The housing crisis is another sore. Victorian Britain built over six million houses between 1837 and 1901. The population was only 18.7 million in 1837 and 37 million by 1901. Today, after decades of dithering, we are told it is simply too difficult to build what we need. The result? Generations still living in their parents' spare room. The dream of home ownership now more elusive than a seat on the Tube at rush hour.

And what of our universities? Once proud engines of inquiry, for those on the right they now resemble neo-Marxist monasteries. The catechism seems to be identity politics and power hierarchies. Questioning this new orthodoxy is heresy. Our youth emerge suspicious of capitalism, uncertain of their freedoms, and convinced that Britain is little more than a villain's mask in history's play.

Meanwhile, the welfare state—once a noble safety net—has become unaffordable. The number of people on permanent disability has risen dramatically after the Covid years. Seems strange. Britain is not rich as many assume. In fact, it is nearing bankruptcy. The cost-of-living crisis tightens its grip, yet benefits balloon and taxes climb. The working Briton is squeezed until the pips squeak. Duty, once a badge of honour, now too often feels like a mug's game.

And the police? Once famed for even-handed fairness, they now seem more eager to police speech than streets. Burglaries unsolved, stabbings unchecked. But heaven help you if your Facebook post ruffles someone's feathers. "Community cohesion" has become the fig leaf for timidity—a polite excuse for inaction—while ordinary Britons feel unprotected and unheard.

Crime spirals. Potholes deepen. NHS waiting times stretch on. Taxes rise while trust falls. The country looks as if it's being run not on values, but on focus groups consensus, improvisation and fear of offence.

The chaos in public policy isn't random. It flows from the same absence: the values that once infused everything we did are now hidden in a cupboard, as if we are ashamed of them. Instead of reaching for them as a compass, leaders have locked them away. Cowed by voices insisting Britain was never great, only cruel, they flinch from their own inheritance.

The irony is this: the very values that once defined Britain are the antidote to the cause of the shrill chorus of discontent. Without them, we wobble. With them, we led for centuries as a beacon of civilisation.

When courts stretch "rights" into unrecognisable shapes, when single-issue quangos and regulators answer to nobody, the betrayal is not by the people, but by the very organs meant to serve them.

And then comes the final insult: to try and "re-educate" the British public with a list of values they don't recognise. As if Britain's history, with its charters, reforms, and bulldog resilience, could be replaced with a few bullet points in a Department for Education memo. It's King Canute on the beach all over again—waving his hands at the incoming tide, convinced a PowerPoint presentation will stop it rolling in.

Worse, this framing quietly shifts blame. If the public no longer trust politicians, it is not because they no longer hold British values. It's the other way around. It is because politicians themselves are no longer seen to represent British values. Specifically, YouGov reported the UK government approval rating falling to a net **-61** in mid-September 2025 (11% approve, 72% disapprove). There's something in that.

Britain needs more than anodyne platitudes or wallpapering over government failure—by parties both on the left and the right. It needs a list. Clear, distinct, lived, defendable. Not quirks, not vibes, not moods—values. And since no one else has done it, as an immigrant, I shall. Nine values. The real thing. Britain's inheritance, written plainly at last.

We have reached a turning point. Do we continue to stumble, apologising for a past distorted beyond recognition? Or do we lift our eyes again to what Britain achieved? This is not nostalgia. It is survival. A nation that forgets its values loses its soul. A nation that reclaims them can lead again. The choice is stark, and the world and its leaders are watching.

2 Nine, Not "Nice"
The Values that Shaped Great Britain

It may feel a little like giving away the score of the match before you've had the chance to watch the game play out. But in the end, it seemed better to put the values up front. That way, as you read the chapters on Britain's history, its missteps, and its astonishing achievements, you'll have a lens through which to see them.

You may be asking yourself what exactly are a country's values? Where do they come from? What happens if they're rotten or produce terrible results? And is there one country, more than any other, whose values other countries have imitated?

Values sit at the bedrock, like the foundations of a house. Culture is then the expression of those values: it builds the walls, turning values into recognisable social habits, the things non-Britons notice first. They only make sense because of the structure beneath. Waiting your turn patiently, saying "sorry" when someone else bumps into you, or keeping your voice down on the train aren't values themselves. They're habits born of deeper commitments to order, politeness, and fairness.

So, when we talk about Britain's nine values, we're talking about the foundations—the deepest foundations of British society that explain why the culture looks and feels the way it does, and why the national habits are so recognisably "British".

The Nine British Values in Essence (*and their Opposites*)

1. **Fair Play for All: One law, one rulebook, no exceptions**
    Not privilege, queue-jumping, rules applied differently to different people and bent for the powerful or special interest groups.

2. **The Free Individual: Liberty to think, speak, and chart one's own individual course**
    Not conformity to clan, crowd, or creed.

3. **Suspicion of Power: Question every throne, title, or ministerial promise**
    Not blind obedience or worship of authority.

4. **Joining In the British Way: Belonging through making an effort, showing up, mucking in, and sharing the load**
    Not isolating in social bubbles or demanding inclusion and respect without contributing.

5. **Owning Our Mistakes: Fail, admit, fix, and move forward in daylight**
    Not denial, delays, cover-up, or rewriting the record.

6. **Duty Before Self: Respect for those who serve beyond themselves**
    Not entitlement, self before others, or ducking responsibility.

7. **Humour in Hardship: Laugh first, complain later, and keep the spirit unbroken**
    Not wallowing in victimhood or weaponising grievance.

8. **Evolution, Not Revolution: Change is by report, debate, and reform, not barricades**
    Not utopian shortcuts, violent spasms, or grand overnight schemes.

9. **Pushing Boundaries: An island forever testing limits, inventing, and exploring**
    Not retreat, stagnation, or hiding from the world.

There is no such thing as a country without values. Even if you tried to invent one, it would quickly develop its own. A nation without values would be like a pub with no beer: technically possible, but functionally unthinkable.

How come one country's values can be very different to the next? Every country ends up with its own set of values, and not by accident. They're hammered out by wars, famines, emperors, revolutionaries, and the general muddle of history.

For the French it is *liberté, égalité, fraternité*, which can still evoke the drama of a street protest. The Japanese elevate politeness to an art form. Bowing isn't just being superficially polite, it is a national ballet of respect. Thailand's gift is grace: a culture of smiles and courtesy so powerful that it makes even the most frazzled visitor pause and breathe and respond in kind, hands clasped together. And Brazil? A national value could be joy in life itself—the belief that life, however messy, should always find room for music, football, and dance.

Universal values sound lovely—until they land in someone else's soil. Nations don't easily swap out the habits they paid for in blood, sweat, and bread rations. Try telling the Swiss to embrace disorder, or the Japanese to live without courtesy, and you'll get nowhere fast. People cling to their values because they remember the cost of getting them. The bigger the cost, the more entrenched the value.

And Are There Bad Values?

Of course, not every country's entrenched values produce happy results for them or for visitors. If your national habits leave you with grinding poverty, sky-high infant mortality, rampant corruption, and life expectancy that makes a pension scheme redundant, then perhaps it's time for leaders to ask whether their country's values belong to a previous era and not now. To not think that is to give up on humanity itself, the idea that we can always move forward and build a better life for every generation.

And many countries have asked that very question. When it came to reinventing themselves, they didn't usually borrow from the Mongol horde, the Spanish Inquisition, or Nazi Germany. No, they cribbed their notes from Britain.

For all its eccentricities—the tea breaks, the weather obsession, the hedgerows—Britain managed to invent a set of powerful civic habits that turned out to be remarkably exportable. Parliaments, courts, limitations on leaders' power, and even that elusive balance between freedom and order: all copied, tweaked, and passed off abroad.

It is, frankly, indisputable. If imitation is the sincerest form of flattery, then Britain has been flatteringly plagiarised for centuries. The world may not like to admit it, but when it comes to creating a prosperous, contented, well-run country, most roads lead not to Rome—but to Westminster.

Now that the values are on the table, the question is simple: what exactly did they do for Britain? The answer lies in Britain's record. This small island managed to shape the modern world far more than its size should have allowed. From engines to empire, from Parliament to penicillin, the story of Britain's achievements is best understood as the story of these values in action and the fruits they produced.

3 The Island That Changed Humanity
Britain's Astonishing Achievements

For a nation that claims it doesn't like to boast, Britain has left a suspiciously long trail of inventions, institutions, and ideas.

Industry and Invention

James Watt's engine of the 1770s turned steam into horsepower, draining mines, powering factories, driving ships, and sending trains clattering across the countryside at speeds that made passengers wonder if their lungs could withstand the velocity. James Hargreaves' spinning jenny of 1764 let one worker spin several threads at once, transforming textiles and making Britain the world's clothier. Edmund Cartwright's power loom of 1785 mechanised weaving, multiplying production and making Luddites furious enough to smash it with hammers. These machines didn't just change how people worked—they changed where they lived, moving millions from field to factory and igniting the Industrial Revolution.

The railway stitched towns together, made coal cheap, and gave birth to seaside holidays. Frank Whittle's jet engine of 1937 shrank the Atlantic crossing from days to hours. And in 1989 Tim Berners-Lee knitted together the World Wide Web, opening every corner of knowledge, opinion, and cat video to anyone with a connection.

Medicine and Health

Science reshaped medicine, often by accident. In 1928 Alexander Fleming left his lab in a mess, went on holiday, and came back to find mould had killed bacteria on his plates. Penicillin had arrived—and millions of lives were saved because a Scotsman didn't tidy up. Over a century earlier Edward Jenner noticed milkmaids rarely caught smallpox, and in 1796 he pioneered vaccination, beginning the end of one of humanity's worst killers. Joseph Lister's antiseptic surgery of the 1860s ended the bloody-apron-as-badge era. Florence Nightingale, armed with soap, discipline, a caring attitude and statistics, turned nursing into a profession during the Crimean War. And in 1948, in a country still rationing bread, Britain founded the NHS, declaring healthcare should be free for all Britons at the point of use.

Economics, Finance and Enterprise

Before Adam Smith, markets were instinct; after him, they were economics. He taught that prosperity doesn't need kings—only markets. Britain built the plumbing of modern capitalism. The joint-stock company, pioneered by the East India Company of 1600, let ordinary investors invest in voyages without losing everything if the ship sank. The Bank of England of 1694 gave governments a place to borrow (and borrowers a place to sweat). The Amicable Society of 1706 launched life insurance, which sounded grim but proved useful.

Law and Politics

In 1215, the barons staged history's most awkward contract negotiation and made King John autograph Magna Carta: proof that even monarchs can be strong-armed into ticking the terms and conditions. Out of medieval councils grew Parliament, the "mother of parliaments", where leaders are still jeered, questioned, and skewered. Trial by jury, habeas corpus (the ultimate anti-kidnapping spell), and equality before the law became global cornerstones. Britain's constitutional monarchy, mocked as pomp and ceremony, turned out to be the most durable safeguard against tyranny—a crown that reigns but does not rule.

Moral Leadership

Britain abolished the slave trade in 1807 and slavery itself in 1833. Then, at vast expense, it sent the Royal Navy to patrol the seas, seizing slave ships and freeing their human cargo. The loans to do this were only finally paid off in 2015! The vote was extended step by step: to all men, then to women. Universal education was created. Trade unions were legalised. The welfare state was built. Other nations staged revolutions with guillotines; Britain reformed with bills in Parliament and patience.

Agriculture and Sport

Jethro Tull's seed drill of 1701 sowed seed in neat rows instead of scattering it. Crop rotation and selective breeding doubled yields and fattened livestock. The result was a fed population ready to power industry. Meanwhile, Britain gave the world football, rugby, cricket, tennis, golf, and squash. Where peasants once chased pigs, Britain gave rules, referees, and proper kit. Football and tennis became global passions. Golf, once banned as a distraction from archery, spread from Scotland to the world. And squash, born from a punctured ball at Harrow in the 1830s, is now played from Cairo to Kuala Lumpur.

Homes and Cities

Victorian terraced houses rose by the mile, red-brick and sash-windowed, from London to Melbourne to Cape Town. Built with near-factory precision—standardised parts, repeated designs, even early forms of prefabrication—they turned housing into mass production. They weren't glamorous, sometimes not even plumbed, but they were sturdy and recognisable, still shaping city streets across continents. London also lit the world's streets: first with oil lamps in the 17th century, then gas lamps in the 19th, and finally electricity. By 1814 Westminster had hundreds of gas lamps while much of Europe relied on moonlight.

Compassion and Culture

In 1822 Parliament passed the first animal welfare law, protecting cattle, horses, and sheep. Two years later came the RSPCA, the world's first animal welfare organisation. At the same time, Britain's cultural reach was astonishing: Shakespeare, Milton, Dickens, Austen, Rowling; Turner, Constable; Elgar, Vaughan Williams; the Beatles, Stones, Queen, Adele, Coldplay. Britain invented the modern novel, the detective story, political satire, and fantasy epic. Even the BBC, at its peak, became a gold standard for broadcasting.

Science and Discovery

Newton gave the laws of motion, calculus, the reflecting telescope, and optics. Faraday discovered electricity and magnetism's link, giving us motors and dynamos. It is easy to forget Ernest Rutherford who spent his life taking things apart that nobody else could even see. He discovered the atomic nucleus by lobbing atomic tennis balls at a gold leaf and suddenly realising there was a pavilion hiding in the middle. He worked out radioactive half-life too, proving that elements don't live forever, they just quietly fade away, like politicians after an embarrassing scandal. He named alpha, beta, and gamma radiation. He split the atom in Manchester in 1917—without a safety manual—and in doing so, laid the groundwork for nuclear power.

Alan Turing cracked the Enigma machine—a fiendish German contraption that spent its days turning plain words into gibberish, until Turing turned gibberish back into victory. He shortened the war, and invented computer logic. Stephen Hawking peered into black holes and became a global icon. Watson (an American) and Crick's 1953 model of DNA—made possible by Rosalind Franklin's famous "Photo 51"—was biology's Rosetta Stone. Dorothy Hodgkin unlocked the structures of insulin and penicillin. John Logie Baird invented television. Oddness, in Britain, has always been the prelude to genius.

Global Impact

In 1940, Britain stood alone against tyranny, endured the pounding of London with 43,000 people dying and 50,000 injured in the Blitz. And then rallied the world. After victory, it dismantled its empire mostly peacefully, creating the Commonwealth. It left behind railways, universities, courts, government institutions and parliaments: tools for potential growth, prosperity and well-being for citizens, not just ruling.

English became the world's language. Nearly 60 sovereign states use it officially, over 80 including territories. In Africa, nearly half the continent's nations conduct their parliaments, courts, and classrooms in English—a legacy of empire that means a Ghanaian lawyer can debate a Kenyan minister without either needing a translator. In the Caribbean and Central America, small island states from Belize to Barbados use English as their glue, while in the north, Canada makes it co-equal with French and the United States runs on it by sheer force of habit.

India and Pakistan keep English as the common ground between their own dozens of languages; Sri Lanka calls it the "link language". Across the Pacific, nearly every island nation from Fiji to the Solomons to Vanuatu keeps English in its constitutional toolbox—a lingua franca scattered like pearls across thousands of miles of ocean.

Back in Europe, of course, English is at home in Britain and Ireland, and despite Brexit, remains the language in which Brussels drafts half its communiqués. That is a kind of irony: the language of the country that left is now the one the European Union cannot leave behind.

A language once confined to a soggy island has become the world's paperwork, its diplomacy, and its small talk at airports.

And perhaps that's the ultimate punchline: Britain lost an empire, but English became the one thing the whole planet adopted—the language in which Japanese pilots talk to French air-traffic controllers while flying over Brazil. Britain may have lost an empire, but it gained a planet full of ESL (English as a Second Language) students.

Conclusion

Britain's record is extraordinary. No other nation has contributed so much, across so many fields, over so many centuries, with such a consistent tilt toward liberty, fairness, and invention. Other nations had bursts of brilliance—Greece with philosophy, Rome with law, Italy with Renaissance art, France with fashion and cuisine, America with mass production and Hollywood. Britain's genius was different: not an isolated flash, but a centuries-long habit of invention, reform, and moral clarity.

While others carved colonies chiefly for plunder, Britain built the hardware of states—railways, schools, institutions, parliaments— and, more importantly, coded them with the software of liberty and common law. Achievements are impressive, but they raise a question: how did a damp island, half the size of Texas, manage to lead the world at all?

Britain's achievements can look like a string of miracles—steam engines, penicillin, Shakespeare, the NHS, the Beatles, and even the World Wide Web. But none of it just "happened". Each breakthrough came out of centuries of muddle and mayhem: arguments in taverns, laws drafted and scrapped, kings beheaded, parliaments patched up, and plenty of wrong turns along the way.

Chapter Three showed the glittering results; Chapter Four takes us into the workshop, where the real mess was made. What seems obvious now was anything but at the time. Britain was improvising, lurching forward, tripping, correcting, and somehow stumbling into greatness. And remember—there was no roadmap: *no empire, civilisation, or kingdom had left instructions for how to build a fairer and freer society. Britain had to invent it all from scratch. It is difficult being the first.*

If we're still puzzled why the rest of the world keeps borrowing Britain's tricks perhaps it's time we retraced the very odd road that got us here.

4 Forged in Fire and Rain
The Long Making of British Values

The Slow Birth of Nine Values

People sometimes imagine that national values arrive like a memo from head office. The French Revolution declared *liberté, égalité, fraternité* in one go, as though values could be launched like a product line. Then came Napoleon. In Britain, it was never like that. We don't do overnight. We do dialogue, reports, committees, and the occasional muttered compromise. And so, the values that now define Britain did not burst forth in a blaze, but crept out over centuries, blinking into the daylight, sometimes tentatively, sometimes with a roar.

Magna Carta: A Tantrum That Changed the World

Picture it: June 1215, a field by the Thames, banners flapping, knights clanking, and King John sulking like a boy told to share his sweets. He'd lost half of France, annoyed the Pope, taxed his barons to boiling point, and earned the nickname "Bad King John".

The barons, fed up, didn't just stab him and grab power. Being English, they drew up a document—signed, sealed, and properly witnessed. Thus was born Magna Carta.

Now, let's be honest. The 1215 Magna Carta wasn't a soaring declaration of human rights. It was, in truth, a medieval shopping list of grievances. There were clauses about fishing weirs, debts owed to Jews, and how widows should not be forced to remarry. The famous stuff—"no free man shall be imprisoned without due process"—was tucked away among the small print. And it only applied to "free men", which excluded about 95% of the population (women, serfs, peasants, the whole lot).

And yet. Out of this baronial tantrum, something remarkable emerged. For the first time, a king was forced to acknowledge his power was not absolute. He could not simply demand taxes or imprison subjects without legal process. That principle—however narrow at first—was dynamite.

John, of course, had no intention of sticking to it. Within months, he was writing to the Pope to have Magna Carta annulled. But history has a way of ignoring kings' intentions and focusing on good ideas. Over the centuries, Magna Carta was dusted off, reinterpreted, and transformed from a feudal contract into a universal principle.

When Charles I tried his hand at absolutism, Parliament brandished Magna Carta. When Americans drew up their Declaration of Independence in 1776, they quoted it. Even Gandhi invoked it when pressing for Indian rights. A dusty list of barons' complaints became the most famous document in the history of liberty.

Meanwhile, across the Channel, France had nothing comparable. Absolutism reigned. "L'état, c'est moi" Louis XIV famously declared—"I am the state". You can't imagine an English monarch saying that with a straight face. The barons at Runnymede would have laughed him out of the meadow.

While John was forced to sign away his powers in a soggy field at Runnymede, King Philip II of France was busy centralising royal power and Pope Innocent III was launching a crusade against heretics. On the continent: absolutism and fire. In England: accountability and parchment. A striking divergence.

Parliament and the Common Law: Talking It Out

If Magna Carta planted the seed, Parliament watered it. The English had long held moots (Anglo-Saxon town meetings), but the Normans turned them into serious admin. By 1265, Simon de Montfort called what historians hail as the first Parliament, with not just nobles but also knights and burgesses (the medieval version of your town councillor—but with more robes, fewer emails, and a great love of self-importance). It wasn't democracy, but it was a start.

Soon, Parliament became a fixture. Kings begged it for money, argued with it, and discovered it was the one institution they couldn't ignore. While France's Estates-General faded and Spain's Cortes rubber-stamped royal edicts, England's Parliament kept chattering, heckling, and—most importantly—saying "no" to the King.

Alongside it grew Common Law. Judges ruled by precedent, not whim: "What did we do last time?" became the principle. It meant law was consistent, predictable, and—at least in theory—binding on kings as well as commoners. One 13th-century dispute about runaway pigs trashing a garden was decided not by decree but by checking the records. Hardly glamorous, but quietly revolutionary.

The flaw, of course, was exclusion. Parliament spoke for landowners, not peasants, and judges cared more about property than poverty. Still, the habit was set: disputes settled by bargaining and rules, not daggers at midnight.

Meanwhile in Europe, kings and emperors still issued orders that had to be obeyed. Spain had the Inquisition; England had parliamentary committees. Which would you rather face?

The Tudors: Suspicion in Petticoats

On the surface, the Tudors look like autocrats in fancy dress: Henry VIII hacking through wives, Elizabeth I "married" to the kingdom. Yet mistrust of authority was already murmuring. Parliament, though cowed by the Tudors, was not silent. Common law grumbled. Plays poked sly fun while monarchs applauded. The seedlings of future habits survived the costume drama.

Some instincts even grew. The Reformation, though sparked by Henry's power-grab, set loose a new habit of questioning authority. For the first time, ordinary men and women read the Bible in English. Conscience and scripture, not priests, began to shape private thought—an idea that would one day fuel dissent and democracy.

Elizabeth, for all her glittering iconography, ruled by constant negotiation. She styled herself the Virgin Queen but relied on humility as performance—walking among her people, tolerating satire, even laughing at plays that mocked her favourites. Power was exalted, but never fully trusted.

Service beyond self also took root. Gentry, magistrates, and parish officers assumed duties for the realm. Poor laws marked the first national system of relief, embedding the principle that communities owed care to their weakest.

Fairness, too, edged forward. Trial by jury expanded, and despite manipulation, the idea that commoners could judge those higher up the social hierarchy gained traction. Shakespeare mirrored this sense of balance: fools skewering kings, justice voiced by unlikely characters.

Mary I had tried to drag England back to Rome by burning her opponents at the stake. Elizabeth, her half-sister, had the sense to say, in effect: "Both Catholic and Protestant are fine—we're going to stop setting each other alight." It was political genius more than theology, but it kept the peace.

So, while the Tudors strutted in silks and wielded the axe, the deeper current bent towards public duty, fairness, and suspicion of unchecked power. Beneath the pageantry, the roots of a national character thickened.

The Enlightenment: Liberty and Honesty with a Wig On

Fast forward to the 17th and 18th centuries. Here the values gained wigs and gravitas. John Locke spoke of the free individual; Milton thundered about liberty of speech. The Royal Society institutionalised a peculiarly British habit: admit your errors, share your findings, let others poke holes in your theories. Owning mistakes became the basis of modern science. Meanwhile, explorers and merchants were pushing boundaries on the seas—sometimes disastrously, sometimes brilliantly, but always restlessly. Britain was learning to be both bold and self-critical, a rare combination.

The Civil War, the Republic, and the Return of the King

The 17th century was Britain's age of political adolescence: stroppy teenage years of slammed doors, rows with authority, and radical hairstyles.

James I and his son Charles I both believed in the "divine right of kings"—that God himself had crowned them, and Parliament was there to clap politely. Parliament, however, had grown fond of saying "no". When Charles tried ruling without it, raising taxes alone and tinkering with Catholic-style reforms, the country snapped.

Civil war broke out: Cavaliers (royalists with flowing locks and a taste for fine wine) versus Roundheads (Parliamentarians with cropped hair and sermons). It ended with the unthinkable: King Charles tried, convicted, and beheaded. Europe gasped in horror. The English? They published the trial transcripts so everyone could read how a king had been told he wasn't above the law.

Oliver Cromwell's republic followed: disciplined, efficient, and utterly joyless. He banned theatre, Christmas, and maypoles for "ungodly dancing". England became the only country where fun was briefly illegal.

By 1660, the nation had had enough dreariness. The monarchy was restored, bringing back laughter, theatre, and puddings. But it was chastened. This was clear: never again would a king rule unchecked.

The Glorious Revolution and the Bill of Rights

The final showdown with the monarchy came in 1688. James II, Charles's brother, tried the old absolutist tricks again—adding Catholicism into the mix. He baptised his heir Catholic, triggering panic among Protestants who had no desire to return to Rome's orbit.

This time, the English didn't bother with another civil war. They essentially ghosted James II and swiped right on Mary (his daughter) and William, importing a ready-made Protestant power couple from Holland. James fled to France, and the whole affair was so bloodless it was nicknamed the "Glorious Revolution".

What makes 1688 truly "Glorious" is not just the outcome but the absence of blood. Across Europe, regime change meant barricades, massacres, and vendettas. In England, James II slipped quietly away, William and Mary arrived by invitation, and Parliament made them sign a contract: the Bill of Rights (1689). A revolution so quiet it barely ruffled the nation's sense of humour.

William and Mary didn't just take the crown; they accepted conditions. Parliament drew up the Bill of Rights in 1689, a kind of Magna Carta 2.0, but sharper. It guaranteed:

- No taxation without parliamentary consent.
- Free elections and freedom of speech in Parliament.
- Regular parliaments must be held.
- No cruel or unusual punishments.

In short: monarchy was now constitutional. Kings and queens could reign, but they would never again rule unchecked.

With Parliament now supreme under William and Mary's Bill of Rights, power began to tolerate something truly revolutionary—the freedom to talk about it.

The Free Press and the Public Voice

Another quiet revolution happened in 1695: the Licensing Act lapsed. Until then, printing had been tightly controlled. Now, suddenly, anyone could set up a press and start spouting opinions. And they did.

Pamphlets flew off the presses. Newspapers blossomed. Political cartoons mocked everyone from monarchs to ministers. Coffeehouses buzzed with debate. In some ways, it was chaos: seditious plots, libellous rants, and bawdy satire filled the air. But it was also exhilarating: the people now had a voice.

Coffee first arrived in Britain in the 1600s, looking suspiciously like tar, tasting like burnt toast, and immediately hailed as a miracle cure for everything from melancholy to marital fatigue. Within weeks the English, never ones to miss an excuse for a chat, had invented the coffeehouse—a place where you could drink bitterness, argue politics, and pretend to be sober, all for a penny.

London's coffeehouses were nicknamed "penny universities": for the price of a coffee, you could hear the latest pamphlets read aloud and argue with merchants, poets, and politicians. Charles II once tried to shut them down, fearing rebellion. He failed. Britain's democracy was fuelled as much by caffeine and gossip as by parchment and law.

The English discovered they liked arguing in print almost as much as in Parliament. This was the age of Addison and Steele's *Spectator*, Daniel Defoe's political journalism, and even Jonathan Swift's wicked satires. By the 18th century Britain had a culture of free debate unrivalled in Europe.

There were limits, of course. Libel laws grew teeth; printers could be sued. But censorship never fully returned. Compare this to France, where printers risked prison, or Russia, where dissenters risked being sent to Siberia. Britain had stumbled upon the noisy, messy, but vital, ingredient of modern liberty: a free press.

A Balanced Constitution

By the early 18th century, Britain's political system looked oddly modern:

- A monarch who reigned but did not rule.
- A Parliament with real power.
- A legal system grounded in precedent and fairness.
- A press free to mock and criticise.

It wasn't democracy yet—the franchise was still narrow, and corruption was rife—but the framework was astonishing. Montesquieu, the French philosopher, travelling through Britain, marvelled at Britain's "separation of powers". American colonists, decades later, would lift Britain's constitutional tricks wholesale for their own republic.

The side effects? Politics was noisy, often corrupt, and sometimes ridiculous. For all its high ideals, 18th-century politics was gloriously corrupt. Some "rotten boroughs" had only a handful of voters; one famously had none at all. Meanwhile, elections were often fuelled by free beer—candidates bankrupted themselves by bribing voters with barrels of ale.

There wasn't a "Monster Raving Looney Party" per se. But if you'd walked into a coffeehouse in 1650s London, you'd have heard Ranters preaching sinless hedonism, and Fifth Monarchists warning the world would end. Which, frankly, makes "Vote for Insanity—You Know It Makes Sense" sound rather sensible.

But Britain recalibrated: each century brought reforms, broadening who could vote, cleaning up corruption, and adapting the system. Out of this chaos, Britain's institutions held and evolved, proving resilience mattered more than perfection.

Other nations lurched from one extreme to another: absolutism, revolution, dictatorship. Britain muddled, bargained, and joked its way into stability.

From this foundation would grow the next great innovations: abolition of slavery, voting rights for all, social reform, and empire reimagined. But it was in these times, in the 17th century's chaos and the 18th century's balance, that modern government was invented.

The Victorians: Duty in Stiff Collars

By the Victorian age, the values were practically wearing name tags. "Doing your duty" was everywhere—in the civil service, in philanthropy, in that relentless push to build schools, railways, hospitals, and yes, empires. Contributing to society—joining in—took civic form: clubs, societies, guilds, choirs, the Women's Institute with its jam competitions. If you wanted to belong in Victorian Britain, you didn't just sit at home. You joined in. You gave. You helped run the annual fête.

Abolition—The Empire's Finest Hour

Slavery was not Britain's invention. It was the human norm. From the beginning of human existence, from Athens to Rome, Cairo to Calcutta, everybody seemed to think it natural to put captives to work. The Greeks called it civilisation; the Romans called it property rights. Medieval Europe renamed it serfdom—you weren't chained, but you couldn't leave. In indigenous communities in Africa, Asia, and the Americas, prisoners of war were bought, sold, or absorbed into tribes. Conquer, and you kept.

Only in a few odd corners—Arctic villages, desert tribes, remote islands—did slavery fail to take hold, mostly because a captive was just another mouth to feed. Even then, exceptions popped up: Vikings carried thralls, Polynesians kept household slaves. If you're looking for a society untouched by it, you'll find yourself on a windswept atoll or scraping roots in the tundra.

And then, in a twist no empire or people had attempted before, Britain decided slavery was wrong—and abolished it. Not because slaves rose up, but because campaigners like William Wilberforce, Thomas Clarkson, and Olaudah Equiano persuaded Parliament that it was morally wrong. In 1807, Britain outlawed the trade; in 1833, slavery itself. Britain even compensated slave owners with £20 million (40% of the government budget, not paid off until 2015).

The costs were immense—£480 billion in today's money. Planters were furious, merchants whining, taxpayers bled. Yet Britain pressed on, sending the Royal Navy to police the seas, freeing 150,000 Africans, and losing 2,000 sailors to disease and wrecks. It was moral leadership at great expense. Britain was doing the right thing, no matter the cost.

Others lagged. America fought a civil war that killed 700,000 before abolishing slavery. Brazil hung on until 1888. Arab markets lasted into the 20th century. Britain did it first, on principle, and enforced it globally. If ever an empire deserved the phrase "leading the world", this was it.

Incidentally, Wilberforce also had a pet tortoise, Charlotte, which outlived him. A fitting metaphor: slow, stubborn, but victorious.

The Race for Empires

By the late 19th century, the world was crowded with empires. Britain's red patches spread across every continent. France coloured in huge swathes of Africa. Spain and Portugal, though long past their glory days, clung to what they had left, mostly in South America. The Dutch kept their grip on the East Indies. Germany and Italy, late to the table, were scrambling for scraps. Belgium, improbably, had turned into King Leopold II's personal shopping spree in the Congo. Russia sprawled from the Baltic to the Pacific. Even America, while loudly denouncing "Old World empires", was quietly casting hungry eyes on the Pacific and Caribbean.

Then came the conferences. The Berlin Conference (1884–85) was the most notorious: a room full of European statesmen solemnly drawing lines across Africa as though it were a board game. No Africans invited, of course. Bismarck played host, King Leopold of Belgium schemed, and maps were redrawn over cigars and brandy. A few years later, the Brussels Conference of 1890 pretended to deal with the slave trade but mostly arranged better shipping routes for ivory and rubber.

It's easy today to sneer at Britain's part in this story. But here's the rub: had Britain stayed at home polishing its naval buttons, its colonies would simply have been swallowed up by other empires— and those empires had very different track records.

The Three Doors of Fate

History rarely hands out easy choices. For many nations, the lottery of geography and empire boiled down to three doors.

Door One: Carry On as You Are

This meant staying outside the empire game altogether. Noble in principle, but in practice it often translated into endless clan wars, famine every other season, despots perched on shaky thrones, and lifespans so short the phrase "middle age" applied to twenty-five-year-olds. Ethiopia, famously independent, survived European colonisation—but endured centuries of warlords, coups, and famines that made freedom feel a rather mixed blessing.

Door Two: Colonisation by Somebody Else

Plenty of takers here. The Belgians turned the Congo into a private rubber plantation so brutal it halved the population within a generation. The Dutch in Indonesia excelled at extracting nutmeg and tin while the locals remained firmly at the bottom of the economic ladder. The Portuguese built an empire from Brazil to Mozambique but left a legacy of shaky institutions and spectacular inequality. And the French? From Indochina to Algeria to West Africa, their colonial "mission civilisatrice" left behind dictatorships, civil wars, and a deep suspicion of democracy.

Door Three: The British Option

Now, Britain was no saint. It taxed, it traded, it sometimes blundered badly. It was heavy handed at times. Famines in India were worsened by poor policy. The Amritsar massacre in 1919 was a stain on Britain's record. In my country, the Anglo-Boer War saw civilians interned in concentration camps.

But it also left behind things that proved oddly useful: railways, common law, courts, schools, universities, civil service structures, and in some places even functioning parliaments. And what became of Britain's former colonies? Look at **Canada**, a G7 economy with one of the highest living standards in the world. Look at **Australia** and **New Zealand**, both democracies, both prosperous, both exporting not just wool and wine but a way of life envied globally. Look at **Hong Kong**, which flourished as one of the great financial centres of the 20th century. Look at **India**, now the world's largest democracy and after a period of socialism and almost no foreign investment or trade allowed by its government until 1991, is now a rising economic powerhouse. Even small places like **Barbados** and **Mauritius** consistently top regional rankings for stability, education, and human rights. These are not accidents. They are the fingerprints of institutions—common law, free press, parliamentary rule— planted by Britain and adapted by locals.

India's first railway line opened in 1853 between Bombay and Thane. Within 60 years, there were over 30,000 miles of track. Built partly for troop movements and cotton exports, railways also transported grain and transformed Indian life—knitting together a subcontinent in ways no Mughal emperor had ever managed. Britain may have left, but the railways never did.

The Commonwealth Test

Britain's decision to end its colonial interests was driven by its debt after the the Second World War and pressure from the US. The cost of the colonies was enormous. Britain withdrew with dignity and created the Commonwealth: a club of nations, unprecedented in history. Many kept the British monarch as their head of state.

And here's the clincher. Membership of the British Commonwealth is voluntary. No gunboats required. That alone suggests the relationship was more complicated than the cartoon of oppression. If empire had been nothing but chains, surely the last thing anyone would want is a club reminding them of it. Yet the Commonwealth endures, a faint but real echo of Britain's third door. No empire in history turned into a voluntary association of equals. It was Britain's most unlikely—and perhaps most enduring—invention.

By the early 20th century, Britain's empire covered a quarter of the globe. It was the largest political entity in history. And yet, its greatest legacy was not territory or trade, but **institutions and values**.

Even the United States, forged in rebellion, built its constitution on English foundations.

Now contrast that with the French legacy in Indochina (which ended in decades of bloody war), or in much of Africa where coups became the national sport. The Dutch left Indonesia with simmering resentments that exploded into violence. The Portuguese clung so tightly to Angola and Mozambique that their exit caused years of bloody civil war and ended in communist dictatorships. The Germans left Africa with borders that still don't make sense. And Belgium's Congo? Its story is so grisly it still makes modern readers flinch.

Empire is a complicated story. Britain made mistakes—sometimes appalling ones. But unlike other empires, it had the habit of self-correction. It abolished slavery everywhere it was. It admitted errors when they occurred. It shifted colonies to stable self-government rather than clinging until collapse.

The pattern was the same as at home: innovate, stumble, recalibrate, persist. Britain's empire was not just about flags on maps; it was about exporting ideas, institutions, and habits of liberty.

Other empires conquered. Britain built. Other empires collapsed. Britain adapted.

This is why, even today, so many of the world's democracies, parliaments, and legal systems bear a distinctly British stamp. The empire, for all its faults, became the greatest transmission line of liberty in history.

Even countries never colonised directly by Britain often borrowed the template. **Denmark, Norway, Sweden, and Finland** all built systems of law, welfare, and governance that look suspiciously like adaptations of Britain's mix of liberty and order. In other words, Britain was the trailblazer. Others either stumbled into tyranny or borrowed Britain's homework.

So yes, Britain carved up the map along with other colonisers. But the alternative would not have been freedom. It would mostly likely have been a continuation of chaos and poverty, or someone else's empire—and almost certainly worse.

Amritsar

The Amritsar massacre of 1919 was empire at its ugliest. General Dyer ordered troops to fire on thousands of unarmed Indians in a walled garden; nearly 400 died in ten minutes. Outrage in Britain was swift: Churchill called it "monstrous", Parliament investigated, and Dyer was dismissed.

This habit of self-examination set Britain apart. France's massacres in Syria or Algeria went unmentioned; Belgium's Congo horrors were buried. Britain debated its failures openly, lampooned them in cartoons, and tried to reform—from Amritsar to the Boer concentration camps.

Yet self-criticism did not prevent tragedy. India's independence in 1947 was Britain's proudest handover, but partition unleashed chaos: millions displaced, up to a million dead. Proof that even with inquiry and reform, empire's best intentions can run aground where local divisions run too deep as they do until today.

The Edwardians and the Wars: Humour in the Trenches

Soldiers in the First World War, gave humour its most poignant stage. In the trenches, surrounded by mud, lice, and death, the British soldier cracked jokes that would sound indecent anywhere else, but which kept despair at bay. *Humour in hardship* became not a quirk, but a national survival strategy. Jokes like "we're surrounded on all sides—excellent, now we can't miss them".

After the First World War there was no revolution. While Russia spun into Bolshevism, and half of Europe flirted with fascism, Britain muddled through with reforms and coalitions. We never burned down the house—we just complained about the colour of the paint and changed it slowly.

Workers and Rights

The Industrial Revolution dazzled with steam engines and railways but also gave Britain child labour, 12-hour shifts, and slums that Dickens could barely exaggerate. Chimney sweeps as young as six were sent up flues until campaigners like Lord Shaftesbury forced reforms through furious resistance.

Britain's answer to industrial cruelty wasn't revolt but reform: Factory and Mines Acts curbed child labour, unions were legalised, strikes protected. Progress was slow, employers dug in, but rights expanded, wages rose, and safety improved.

Elsewhere, change came with bullets and barricades. In Britain, it came with debates, pamphlets, and Acts of Parliament—a quieter, steadier revolution.

The Culture of Gradualism

Britain's road to democracy was less thunderclap than slow shuffle. In 1832, the vote went to property-owning men with waistcoats;

by 1867, coal-dusted workers joined; by 1884, calloused farmhands too. Women got a toe in the door in 1918, and only in 1928 did every adult finally hold the ballot. Britain's way was to say "no" first, have a long debate about it, then concede gradually—until, eventually, everyone got their turn.

This habit of gradualism was not weakness—it was strength. It allowed Britain to modernise without collapse, to absorb social change without bloodshed. The French Revolution devoured its children; the Russian Revolution enslaved them. The British Revolution never happened, because reform made it unnecessary.

By the early 20th century, Britain had turned from a land of lords and squires into a full democracy. Workers could vote, women could vote, rights were entrenched. Liberty was no longer the privilege of a few but the inheritance of all.

Britain in the Great War: Principle at a Price

In 1914, Britain faced a choice. Germany had invaded Belgium, tearing up treaties like so much scrap paper. Britain could have stayed aloof, safe behind the Royal Navy. Instead, it declared war— not because Belgium was a trading rival or an ally of centuries, standing, but because Britain had promised to defend its neutrality.

It was, at root, a moral choice: honouring a pledge, upholding the principle that treaties matter. "Britain keeps her word," declared Prime Minister Asquith, and so millions of young men marched to the front.

The side-effect was catastrophic. The trenches of Flanders became killing fields. The flower of a generation perished in mud and barbed wire. The Somme, Passchendaele—names etched in grief.

And yet, Britain held to the principle. At Versailles in 1919, it helped redraw Europe, however imperfectly, with an eye to international law and institutions. The League of Nations was born of British and Wilsonian vision, a first attempt at global governance. Britain had demonstrated, for all its losses, that it would fight not just for empire, but for principle.

Britain Alone: 1940

Picture the summer of 1940. France had fallen in six weeks. Hitler controlled Europe from the Atlantic to the Vistula. Only Britain remained, an island fortress, facing the might of the Nazi war machine.

The Luftwaffe launched the Battle of Britain. Night after night, bombs fell on London, Coventry, Liverpool. The Blitz flattened houses, churches, entire streets. And yet the people endured. Tube stations became shelters; jokes were cracked as buildings smouldered. However hard and tragic life had become, humour gave the British relief.

During the Blitz, volunteers from the Women's Voluntary Service drove mobile canteens through bombed-out streets, handing out tea to victims and firemen alike. To foreigners it looked surreal: buildings collapsing, yet people sipping tea. To Britons, it was normal. Resilience flavoured with a teabag.

Churchill's speeches—"we shall fight on the beaches", "their finest hour"—were not mere rhetoric. They were the articulation of a national character: stubborn, resilient, unwilling to yield.

The consequence of Britain sticking to its values was devastation. Cities scarred, children evacuated, rations meagre. But the calibration was persistence. Britain refused to surrender, bought time until America joined and the tide turned.

In doing so, Britain quite literally saved civilisation. Had it fallen, Hitler's empire would have stretched unopposed across Europe. That it did not was due to one island's refusal to bow.

After the Second World War: Belonging and Correction

By 1945, Britain emerged victorious—but exhausted. Two world wars in a generation had drained it of wealth and manpower. The empire, stretched thin, could not last.

In July 1945, weeks after victory in Europe, Winston Churchill was voted out of office. Britons, grateful for his wartime leadership, nevertheless chose Clement Attlee's Labour Party to rebuild peace.

Few nations would dismiss a war hero so briskly. But for Britain, principle mattered more than personality: war was done, welfare was next.

The side-effect of victory was paradoxical: Britain had won but was weakened. America and the Soviet Union were now the great powers. Britain had to recalibrate.

It did so by choosing dignity over denial. Unlike France or Portugal, which clung to colonies until bloody wars forced them out, Britain began a managed retreat. India gained independence in 1947, followed by wave after wave of decolonisation. The process was not perfect but compared to Algeria, Indochina, or Angola, Britain's handovers were relatively peaceful.

The Welfare State: Beveridge's Blueprint

In 1942, as bombs fell, William Beveridge sketched five "giants" to be slain: Want, Disease, Ignorance, Squalor, and Idleness. It read like a medieval quest, but it was the birth of the Welfare State.

After the war, Attlee's Labour government set it in motion: the NHS, wider education, better housing, social security. It was ruinously expensive—Britain was broke and still on rations—yet the principle stuck. No soldier should return to poverty; no child goes untreated for lack of money.

Governments since have tweaked and trimmed but never dismantled it. Even Thatcher, red pen in hand, tiptoed around the NHS. Why? Because fairness, once made universal, proved untouchable.

The NHS, launched in 1948, quickly became a national symbol. Infant mortality fell, life expectancy rose, and Britain found itself with a new kind of patriotism: pride in free healthcare. The queues of first time users, understandable inefficiencies, and dreadful hospital food became the running jokes. But the NHS itself became sacred.

In the end, Britain's welfare experiment showed that reform, not revolution, could deliver fairness. Others offered patchwork or paternalism. Britain went for universality—and, true to form, made it up as it went along.

Lost and Confused

What now? Britain feels like it has misplaced itself. Once a country that stood against the power of kings and Nazis, gave the world habeas corpus, DNA, and even the rules of football, it now seems unable to deliver what its desperate citizens plead for. The trouble runs deeper than policies.

It feels as if leaders have set aside the values that carried Britain through centuries—fairness, free individuals, suspicion of power—and fallen in love with different values, borrowing ideas cooked up in committees in other countries, foreign lecture halls or in ivory towers where nothing practical has ever been tested. Worse, these borrowed values often paint Britain as a malign force, as though abolishing slavery, inventing democracy, and standing alone against Hitler were just exceptions in an otherwise wicked record.

If Britain is malign, one has to ask: compared to whom? The French Revolution that ended in a guillotine shortage? The Soviets who industrialised Siberia with forced labour? To measure Britain against some pristine utopia that has never existed is not idealism; it is childish fantasy dressed up as moral superiority.

Underneath the current malaise, the values that made this country strong are still there—as stubborn as drizzle, as reliable as the shipping forecast. The problem isn't that Britain has no compass, but that it has been persuaded to stop looking at it. Rediscovering those values isn't nostalgic flag-waving; it's practical. They are the tools that built stable government, honest courts, and prosperity that spread far beyond these shores. If Britain stopped trying to impress the world by copying everyone else's example and simply remembered its own, it could lead again—not by shouting about it, but by showing how a free, fair, self-correcting society works in practice.

The growing unrest in Britain isn't just about bills, potholes, or waiting times at A&E. It's about values forged over centuries on which Britons have built their lives and communities—people wanting them back, plain and simple.

The fluttering of St George's flags is not a call to arms, nor a rehearsal for some dark nationalism. It's a signal flare: a quiet people saying, "Hey you, politician, this is who we are, and we'd like it remembered." To dismiss that as dangerous is lazy, and to equate it with bellicose nations of history is a low IQ response. Britons don't march for empire; they hang bunting for fairness, humour, and the freedom to grumble without being told they are hateful because they offended one person in 69.23 million.

After centuries of quarrels, compromises, and a civil war, Britain stumbled into something remarkable: a way of living that kept freedom alive without tearing the place apart. There was no guidebook, no model to copy—we made it up as we went along. What, exactly, did we end up with? Let's have a better look at the nine values.

5 The Nine British Values
What They Are (and Definitely Are Not)

If Britain's history were a musical, it would be less *Les Misérables* (all barricades and doom) and more *Oliver!*—scrappy orphans, dodgy politicians, sudden bursts of song, and just enough pluck to muddle through.

Britain's story so far has been one of astonishing invention and often awkward correction of whatever downside these inventions caused. This habit created the distinctive **British Values** we see today: forged in Magna Carta's baronial stand, honed by Parliament's stubborn survival, tested in colonial contradictions, and made ironclad in the Blitz.

These values weren't imported from another country—they were hammered out on muddy battlefields, in crowded coffee houses, and on factory floors. They are not bumper stickers that can be torn off and replaced, they are DNA. And here they are ...

1. Fair Play for All

No one is above the rules—not kings, not ministers, not billionaires. The law is the referee, and everyone plays under the same rules. Fair play runs deep. Britons can't stand anyone pushing in or taking unfair advantage. And it means something tougher too—not plotting, scheming, or manipulating to take more out of the system than you put in. That's why "tax evaders" or "benefits cheat" are two of the gravest insults in the tabloid lexicon, while "fair cop" is accepted with a shrug. And it goes beyond people—Britain was the first country to pass animal welfare laws, because fair play also means standing up for those who can't stand up for themselves, whether it's the underdog in society or the dog in the animal shelter.

2. The Free Individual

Here you stand as yourself, not as someone's cousin, clan member, or co-religionist. Your rights, and your duties, belong to you as an individual. That freedom means more than legal status: it is the liberty to think aloud, to argue, and to seek truth without fear. It extends even to personal space—the Briton's invisible bubble is as sacred as their front door. That's why a neighbour will tolerate your drum kit in the garage (just) but flinch if you stand too close. Freedom here is not flamboyant, but stubborn: the quiet insistence that each person should be able to say their piece without fear of being shouted down.

3. Suspicion of Power

Britons don't trust anyone who gets too big for their boots. From Magna Carta to Prime Minister's Questions, power is meant to be challenged, never worshipped. Leaders are expected to submit to heckling, satire, and awkward interviews with local radio. No one is above the grilling, whether monarch, minister, duchess or football manager. Unlike some countries, where authority is bowed to, in Britain it is prodded, teased, and generally brought down a peg. That may frustrate rulers and celebrities, but it has kept tyranny at bay for centuries without the need for weapons.

4. Joining In the British Way

Belonging in Britain isn't automatic. It's not about paperwork, accents, or ancestry—it's about effort. You have to join in. You have to make the first move. That might mean turning up at the school fête with a Victoria sponge, volunteering at the food bank, sitting on the Parent Teachers Association, or at the very least putting your name down for the raffle. It's about showing you're willing to share the load, however small, and to respect the rules that keep everyone else free.

At the same time, the promise is generous. In Britain you can do as you like in your own home—paint it pink, cook with seven spices, pray or not pray at all—so long as you accept that once you step outside, you are part of the wider community. The freedom is real, but it rests on reciprocity.

The market square is a place to be pleasant, to interact in small but warm ways. To help without being asked. To wait your turn. To make a joke to a stranger when caught in the rain. To give your umbrella to a someone you may never see again. To help the person in the tented market stall move their goods out of the rain without being asked. To help an older person across the road in the face of impatient motorists. To pay it forward. To give the busker some small change but sometimes ask them to turn down their loudspeaker if it is too intrusive on everyone else's enjoyment. Kindly.

Britons are hurt by those who avoid mixing or isolate themselves in bubbles. They are seen as breaking the promise of what it means to be British. But those who reach out, adapt, and connect—still being uniquely themselves—find an embrace, often more warmly than they expect.

> *I have loved playing the church organ since I was a kid. I did have organ lessons once but regard myself as an imposter. I will use the pedals, but I improvise. I spent many years as a church organist and pianist in our town in Berkshire. After the service, as everyone walked out, I would improvise on the melody of the last hymn. There was one couple who would sit and listen to me until I stopped playing when everyone else had left the building. I asked them once why they sat there and told them I was not actually a good organist. Their answer was "you are the most enthusiastic organist we have ever heard, and we love that". There it was, the appreciation of joining in, doing your best, not having to be perfect.*

Where the American Dream says "make it big", the British version quietly says "muck in". It's humbler, less flashy, but no less powerful:

a social contract that anyone can be British, provided they make the effort to belong.

5. Owning Our Mistakes

Britain gets things wrong—sometimes badly. But unlike most, it has made a habit of correcting itself in public. When mistakes happen, inquiries are launched, failures printed in black and white, and blame handed out with an unsparing flourish. Sometimes it takes too long (see: Bloody Sunday, Windrush, Hillsborough and the "Rape Gangs"), but the principle remains: if we mess up, we eventually face up. This is not common practice worldwide.

Britain, with its odd habit of broadcasting every blunder in triplicate, thinks honesty is a strength. It is messy, often painful, but it has allowed Britain to reset and repair where others descend into denial or revenge. Yet some abroad and at home treat it as weakness, happily ignoring the apology while filing Britain permanently under "villain". Meanwhile, their own country's schoolbooks glide smoothly over massacres, coups, and famines as though they were bank holidays, leaving future generations blissfully ignorant. It grates Britons.

6. Duty Before Self

Doing your bit for others, often at your own expense or when you would rather be doing something else, is a badge of honour. From monarchs to nurses, soldiers to volunteers, those who serve others earn the nation's respect. The Blitz spirit was not about heroics, but about tea-ladies who showed up, milkmen who delivered, and wardens who checked the blackout.

Modern examples abound: the retired doctor who returned during Covid, the pensioner who runs the village charity shop, or the teenager who referees junior football on a Sunday morning or visits strangers in retirement homes to play a game of drafts. These acts may be small, but together they define the British sense that dignity comes not from what you take, but from what you give to others.

One of the most attractive—and least understood—examples is

British kindness. Not the noisy, hash-tagged variety that comes with moral slogans and selfies, but the quiet, almost embarrassed kind that involves actually doing something helpful and then moving briskly on. Someone falls off a bike, and a Briton stops, picks them up, brushes them down, and cycles off again without exchanging names. They help, then they let go.

Now, it's important to say what this kind of kindness isn't. It's not tolerance—which is the art of suffering the neighbour's obsession with their leaf blower each autumn until winter arrives. It's not niceness, that syrupy form of social diplomacy that allows people to say "How interesting" when they mean "How ghastly". Nor is it empathy, which implies sharing another's feelings. The British regard that as invasive, like emotional trespassing. They'd rather repair your puncture and hand you a biscuit. It's not even sympathy, because that involves joining you in your misery, which seems terribly unproductive— someone has to remain calm and carry on. And Britons shy away from compassion the way cats shy away from bathwater. They'll rush to help and mop up—but only so long as no one carries on and on about feelings.

For Britons, handling the hardship of others is much the same as handling their own: quietly, with a little joke. The laughter doesn't mean they don't care; it means they do but can't bear to make a fuss about it. So, they make putting others before themselves look like fun, and the sacrifice look like silliness—a social sleight of hand that keeps compassion bearable and duty cheerful.

These acts may be small, but together they define the British sense that dignity comes not from what you take, but from what you give to others.

7. Humour in Hardship

When things go wrong, Britons reach for a joke before a complaint. It's not denial—it's survival. Laughter keeps the spirit unbroken. From the sardonic graffiti of the trenches ("If you can read this, you're in range") to the lockdown memes about banana bread and toilet rolls, the British reflex is to turn misery into a punchline. It makes hardship bearable, failure forgivable, and disaster survivable. Other nations may see this as flippant. Britons see it as survival and the strength to keep going. The famous "Keep Calm and Carry On" slogan could be "Keep Calm and tell a joke to make us all feel better".

Then there is Red Nose Day. For the uninitiated, it's Britain's annual national charity carnival, a televised marathon of daft stunts and comic sketches in which millions of ordinary people do ridiculous things to raise serious money for people in need.

The genius of Red Nose Day lies precisely in its refusal to be solemn. At its heart, it is a riot of tiny absurdities—people in school uniforms racing shopping trolleys, office staff in tutus shaving off moustaches, entire workplaces baking cakes for strangers—all earning money for serious causes. That blend of silliness and solidarity creates a space where giving to those facing hardship meets British humour: you join in, you laugh, you feel part of something. It's no wonder that the event has raised upwards of £34 million in one night alone in 2025. Over its lifetime it has crossed the "billions-of-pounds" mark in the UK. In a nation that copes with crisis by cracking a joke, Red Nose Day proves that laughter isn't an escape from suffering—it's the British way of wrestling it to the ground with a smile.

8. Evolution, Not Revolution

Britain changes slowly, with endless debates. It can feel maddening, but it avoids the revolutions and bloodshed others have endured. The Reform Acts extended the vote step by step, rather than in one grand convulsion. The monarchy slimmed down, the Lords reformed, the colonies let go, all through argument, compromise, and gradual adjustment. Change here is rarely glamorous, but it lasts. If other nations prefer the drama of civic upheaval, Britain prefers the drip of reform—less exciting, but infinitely less bloody.

9. Pushing Boundaries

An island people who never stayed put. From ships to science to Shakespeare, Britain has always tested limits—exploring, inventing, and daring others to follow. It mapped the stars, split the atom and decoded DNA. Curiosity and contrariness combine: if told something cannot be done, Britons will try anyway. The results have not always been perfect, but they have been extraordinary. The world today—its laws, science, arts, and freedoms—bears Britain's fingerprints in every corner.

A Deeper Understanding

A value is only truly understood when you see its shadow. *Fair Play* makes sense the moment you see the pub quiz team smuggling in their phones under the table. *The Free Individual* only shines when set against the suffocating family or community collective that insists you do as you're told. *Suspicion of Power* is clear enough when someone salutes the loudest voice in the room, even if it's spouting nonsense. And *Joining In*? It's not just raffles and Victoria sponges— it's the antidote to sulking in the corner, shouting your own rules, demanding respect, or painting graffiti to mark your territory.

By pairing each value with its opposite, we cut through the fog of those well-intentioned clichés like "tolerance" or "niceness". Values are not like sympathy card sentiments; they are rules of life, hammered out in history, and fought over with clear boundaries. Britain's genius is not just having values but knowing what they are **not**—and saying so plainly, even with a raised eyebrow and a touch of humour.

We will now explore each value in turn by considering its opposite.

1. Special Privilege vs. Fair Play

What Britons cannot stand is the whiff of double standards. The local councillor who thinks parking fines are for others. The official who waves rules for a chum. The loudmouth who pushes to the front. In Britain, unfairness isn't just irritating—it corrodes trust. Cheat the system, even in small ways, and you don't just break the law, you break the bond.

2. The Collective Cage vs. The Free Individual

The opposite instinct is to treat people as mouthpieces for a tribe, party, clan, or religion. Your opinions are assumed, your freedoms curtailed, your choices made by others. Britons find this suffocating. The idea that one must shout the approved slogan, or that loyalty to blood trumps loyalty to conscience, jars deeply. Here, even eccentricity is defended, because the individual—not the group—is the real unit of freedom.

3. Blind Obedience vs. Suspicion of Power

Other lands cheer their leaders, salute their generals, and hang portraits of rulers in classrooms. Britain sharpens its pencils for satire. Blind obedience is alien here. Too much deference and something feels off. Power without scrutiny breeds abuse, Britons know this and instinctively reach for irony when others bow. If your ruler expects worship, Britain will supply mockery instead.

4. Standing Apart vs. Joining In

The anti-value here is withdrawal. Not mucking in but walling off. Groups that live as if the rest of the country doesn't exist, keeping their own rules, their own spaces, grate against the British grain. Equally grating is the loud demand to have everything changed to suit one's own taste while giving nothing back. To belong in Britain, you must be the one to stick your hand up and volunteer, even if you don't know what it's for. To stand aloof, or to demand exceptions and special treatment, is to miss the point entirely and is completely un-British.

5. Denial and Blame vs. Owning Our Mistakes

Some cultures bury errors, hide or destroy archives, or point the finger elsewhere. Britons, by contrast, dig into their own failures with committees, inquiries, and late-night satire. The refusal to admit mistakes is not seen as strength but as weakness—cowardice dressed up as pride or honour. Nothing annoys a Briton more than a cover-up; if there's muck, they'd rather rake it out in the open than leave it festering.

6. Indifference vs. Duty Before Self

And if kindness is the unspoken oil in the British engine, then its absence explains why so many Britons now feel like strangers in their own land. The opposite of kindness, in the British sense, is not cruelty. It's *indifference*—the shrug, the blank stare or averted eyes, the silence in the lift, the bureaucratic voicemail that says "your call is important to us" before cutting you off. It's the automated "no" instead of the human "let me see what I can do".

The effect is subtle but corrosive. When small kindnesses disappears, public life hardens. Once, it was the default setting: the bus driver waiting an extra few seconds for the pensioner, the stranger carrying your suitcase up the station steps. Now one suspects the driver fears a complaint and the stranger fears suspicion.

7. Self-Pity vs. Humour in Hardship

The opposite reaction to adversity is complaint, grievance mongering, and especially performative outrage and melodrama. Some cry conspiracy; others wallow in victimhood. Britons prefer gallows humour. To respond to every difficulty with outrage or despair is to miss the protective power of a joke. For Britons, laughter in the dark isn't flippant—it's the torch that lights the way. Without it, hardship becomes heavier, and resilience drains away.

8. All-or-Nothing vs. Evolution

Some nations throw up roadblocks, storm palaces, or rewrite constitutions overnight. Britain prefers discussion and slow amendments. The opposite impulse—ripping everything up in a frenzy—is viewed as idiotic, childish, petulant and dangerous. Sudden upheaval rarely ends well. Britons are maddened by delay, but they also know that rash revolutions devour their children. Better the boring report than the blood-soaked street.

9. Fear of Risk vs. Pushing Boundaries

Some societies cling to the safe and familiar, refusing to question, refusing to test. Britons itch to experiment, to poke, to prod. What jars is timidity—the refusal to try for fear of failing, the suspicion of curiosity as dangerous, the habit of clipping wings before they can stretch. If Britain had settled for caution, it would never have sailed, never have invented, never have discovered. Without risk, there would have been no Newton, no jet engine, no World Wide Web—only a nation staring at its own shoes. The British don't see life as fate to be accepted but as an ongoing group project—repainting civilisation one step at a time.

Are Some Values More Important Than Others?

Not all values weigh the same on Britain's scales. Some are granite pillars, others more like polished brass fittings. *Fair Play* comes first because without it nothing else works; a nation that lets queue-jumpers run riot cannot hope to govern a country or even a bus stop.

The Free Individual follows close behind, because Britain has always insisted that the "I" matters before the "we". When "we" does matter, it is not focussed on family and clan, it is with everyone beyond that, *Joining In the British Way* with strangers because they are fellow citizens. *Suspicion of Power* is the watchdog snarling in the corner; it never sleeps, so it belongs near the top.

Owning Our Mistakes and *Duty Before Self* sit in the sturdy middle: they're the ballast, the weight in the keel. Without them, Britain would topple at the first puff of scandal or the first leaf on the railway line. *Humour in Hardship* might seem like a luxury, but when everything else cracks, the joke is the glue. *Evolution, Not Revolution* is Britain's quiet superpower: the ability to muddle through by committee until the guillotines rust. And finally, *Pushing Boundaries* takes the rear guard—not because it is least, but because it is the restless itch that keeps Britain moving when it might otherwise sit down to watch daytime TV and stay there forever.

So yes, the values are all important, but some bite harder, some soothe better, and some simply make us laugh when everything else goes wrong.

The truth is that Britain's values are not optional extras. They are hard-won, centuries deep. *Fair Play for All* means the same rules apply whether you are for the government or against it. *The Free Individual* means you don't police speech with dishonest "we want to preserve community cohesion" gags which no one buys any more, while shouting down dissent. *Suspicion of Power* means you don't hand authority to quangos or Brussels-lite bureaucracies with no accountability. *Joining In* means newcomers adapt to Britain, not the other way round. *Duty Before Self* means politicians serve the people, not their careers, not their think tanks, not their post-politics consultancies.

Even more, *Owning Our Mistakes* means admitting where policies fail, not spinning until the public turns green with nausea. *Humour in Hardship* means laughing together through difficulty, not sneering at the voters' worries. *Evolution, Not Revolution* means steady reform, not wild U-turns every few months. And *Pushing Boundaries* means genuine innovation, not virtue-signalling schemes that cost billions while potholes remain unfilled.

The British may endure much, but they do not endure being played for fools. These values are the grain of the nation. Saw across them, and the splinters fly. Govern with them, and the wood shines. Ignore them, and the fury of the people will not be soothed by slogans, gimmicks, or another international conference selfie.

But values are not meant to live in dusty manifestos or in the mouths of politicians who remember them only at election time. They live in waiting your turn at the post office, in the jokes at funerals, in the way neighbours swap keys before holidays, and in the instinctive frown when someone takes liberties. If you want to see them, you don't go to a lecture hall. You look out the window, walk down the high street, or watch a village fête unfold in all its glory. In the next chapter, we'll step into that world—the bells, the market square, and yes, even the cricket pitch—where British values are not argued but lived.

6 The Bells, the Market Square, the Cricket Pitch
How Values Shape the Sights and Sounds of Britain

Britain's values are not hidden in law books. They are audible in bells, visible in hedgerows, tangible in markets and terraces. You can walk through them, sit beneath them, or taste them with jam on a scone. And you notice them most clearly when you glimpse their opposites—the sights and sounds of places that have chosen a different path.

1. Fair Play for All

In Britain, the church bell rings the same note for duke and dustman. The cricket match is settled by the umpire's word. The public footpath cuts firmly through a private estate.

In other lands, you hear a different sound: the cry of protest when the referee's decision can be bought; a gate being locked against passers-by. Even animals are tools or status symbols, not companions. In some village squares, the "rule" is whatever the local strongman says it is, enforced with a shrug. In parts, bribery is as routine as buying a tram ticket. And in the Anglosphere cousins abroad, "mates' rates" or "old boys' clubs" sometimes still trump equal rules for all. To Britons, this all feels like someone cheating—

not a crime exactly, but enough to trigger that tut which cuts deeper than words.

2. The Free Individual

The terraced street tells the story: neat rows, each with a modest door, each signalling a life lived by choice. The snug pub hums with voices. Everyone is free to grumble about the weather, the council, or the Prime Minister. The landlady's bell at last orders is the only censor.

And then there is the invisible bubble. On a crowded island, space is rationed—yet every Briton carries their own air around them. On platforms, waiting to check out at the grocery store, even in pubs, a certain distance is observed. No leaning in. No breath on the neck. Stand too close, and you trespass without stepping inside their home.

Elsewhere, closeness might signal warmth or solidarity. Here, it feels like intrusion. It's a small land mass and one of the most crowded in Europe—and even in the world. The Briton doesn't shove back, only shuffles politely away. But the recoil says everything: freedom means the right to your own space, however small.

This instinct for individuality is also why the face and voice matter so deeply in Britain. Britain prizes the dignity of the person, with the face and voice as signs of individuality. A handshake, a nod, a wry smile about the rain—these are the small exchanges that make public life work. Concealing self-expression runs against the grain of the British "front door" principle, where each person signals their independence, however modestly.

> I wore sunglasses a lot when I first came to the UK. A South African habit. I found the light grey sky hurt my eyes. A colleague told me to remove them because I looked like a gangster, dodgy and unprofessional. British clients would not approve: hiding my eyes would be perceived as creating distance in what should be a courteous exchange. Belonging in Britain is demonstrated through shared gestures: the smile in the shop, the nod in the street, the joke about the weather. Obscuring one's individuality can unintentionally disrupt those small signals of common life.

3. Suspicion of Power

The market square is a theatre of gossip and mockery. A mayor's foibles are discussed as loudly as the price of fish. A cartoonist in Fleet Street scrawls donkey ears on the Chancellor and sells more papers for it.

Beyond our shores, the square may be silent, watched by guards. The cartoonist's pen is turned to flattery. The sound is not heckling but chanting—rehearsed and approved—the sound of intimidation instead of dissent. In North America, power often hides behind expensive consultants and a smile so polished it blinds. In Britain, by contrast, we mock our leaders the moment they rise—"too posh", "too slick" or "too slippery". It is not cruelty; it is insurance. *Suspicion of power* is the national emergency brake.

4. Joining In the British Way

The Women's Institute cake sale, the scout hut, the village fête tombola—each a token of belonging. The sound of coins clinking in a charity tin is the gentle proof of membership: give a little, be part of the whole.

Abroad, the square is crowded but divided, groups standing apart, speaking only among themselves. The sound is of parallel lives—loud with assertion but quiet in contribution. Belonging is claimed but not earned. In parts of North America, identity politics sometimes pulls groups further apart; in Eastern Europe, neighbourly suspicion still lingers across old fault-lines: "Are you with us or with Moscow?" Britain prizes the unshowy "muck in": help clean up the local stream, help build a children's playground, join the rota at the football club. It may look trivial, but it is glue. Without it, everyone retreats to their own corner, and the hum of shared life falls silent. We cease to sound like a country.

5. Owning Our Mistakes

Britain holds inquiries. Documents pile high, apologies are printed, and politicians shuffle out of office "to spend more time with family". Everyone sees through it, but the ritual matters.

In foreign parts, the silence after a disaster may be deafening. Mistakes are covered with banners. Blame is shouted at outsiders. The sound is a strident denial that convinces no one but must still be repeated. The past is not admitted; it is erased. In parts of Southern Europe, corruption scandals rumble on for decades without consequence. In Eastern Europe, whole episodes vanish from the record like chalk washed away by rain. In Britain, the Chilcot Inquiry into our role in the Iraq War lasted seven years, cost £13 million, and still managed to tell everyone what they already suspected. It was maddeningly slow, but at least the truth was typed, bound, and left on the shelf for anyone to read.

6. Duty Before Self

An NHS nurse cycles through drizzle. The poppy seller rattles a tin as the evening cold draws in. A rambler clears a path she may never walk again. Ordinary duty, unheralded, is the background hum of British life.

In other countries, the duty may stop at the threshold of the home. The sound within is of family demanding loyalty; the sight outside is of public neglect, shared spaces crumbling while private walls are painted fresh. In Eastern Europe, duty is sometimes still coloured by memories of forced labour, leaving citizens wary of anything that smells of obligation. The British way is different: duty is chosen, not coerced, and is respected precisely because it is quiet and often anonymous. It is the snow shovelled from the neighbour's path, the litter picked up in the park when no one is watching, the checking in on elderly neighbours to see if they are OK or need anything done.

7. Humour in Hardship

It's become a running joke that "a proper British summer" includes a picnic under rain umbrellas. During the Second World War, Londoners would paint witty signs on bomb-damaged buildings. For example, outside a half-collapsed pub, a chalkboard read, "More open than usual".

Then there are the everyday letdowns: If the kettle breaks: "Well, civilisation has collapsed. Back to the Dark Ages". A flat pint of beer: "Ah, the authentic wartime experience". The post not arriving: "Royal Mail—still preserving the element of surprise". Spike Milligan (born in India) famously has "I told you I was ill" engraved on his gravestone, which sums up the tradition perfectly.

In other parts of the world hardship brings solemnity or loud protest—riots in the streets or sullen endurance. The sound is never laughter. To laugh at one's own plight would be unthinkable. In Germany, gallows humour has never quite gained social respectability; in Russia, irony is whispered rather than broadcast. In America, complaint is a constitutional right. But in Britain, the laugh at adversity is a quiet weapon. The boiler breaks, the roof leaks, the train is late— "could be worse", someone mutters, and everyone chuckles. It doesn't fix the problem, but it fixes the mood and makes the hardship bearable.

8. Evolution, Not Revolution

The hedgerow trimmed. The town clock ticking. The committee plodding through its minutes—slow, steady, undramatic. The sound of continuity is often quiet but enduring.

Elsewhere, the landscape is built one month and demolished the next, new monuments rising before the dust of the old has settled. The sound is of slogans chanted in the street, followed by silence when the next ruler arrives. Britain's tut is a very different music from that of marching boots. Southern Europe's revolutions have left flags and martyrs, but often little continuity. Eastern Europe swapped one ideology for another at dizzying speed. The Anglosphere, too, has its shocks: political earthquakes every four years, systems rebooted with each new administration. Britain may grumble about its committees, but it prefers plodding on to tearing down.

9. Pushing Boundaries

Ships sail from Portsmouth. Satellites launch from Cornwall. Shakespeare is reinvented. Punk rattled the windows of polite society. The sounds are experimental, cheeky, insistent—a refusal to sit still.

Beyond our shores, boundaries are walls, not challenges. The sound is of conformity: voices lowered, steps cautious, fate accepted, silence where innovation should be.

In some places, pushing too far brings exile, or worse. In Britain, it brings a knighthood—or a weary tut. In Eastern Europe, science was once shackled by politics, discoveries delayed or hidden. In parts of the Anglosphere, innovation is welcome but often monetised into the ground before it matures. Britain has always given space to the oddball experimenter: the eccentric tinkerer in the shed, the playwright tearing up language, the band bringing Eastern religions to the West. Sometimes it fails spectacularly. But when it works, it shifts the world.

In private, Britain gladly hosts the sights and sounds of many cultures: spices in the kitchen, unfamiliar rhythms behind closed doors. **But public space is different**. It is the visible and audible stage on which British values are lived. Change that stage too radically—with proclamations intoned instead of bells chiming the day away, with streets crowded by jostling assertion rather than shared belonging—and you alter the values themselves. British public life has always been quieter, gentler, threaded through with compromise and humour. To lose that is to lose the scenery of freedom.

Britain's scenery of values—the bells, the greens, the terraces, the hedges—is not just quaint nostalgia. It is the lived expression of habits that took centuries to form: fairness, freedom, suspicion of power, mucking in, owning up, public duty, gradual reform, humour, proceeding carefully with change and boldness. They are so familiar to Britons that they are scarcely noticed, like background music. But when other sights and sounds intrude—louder, harsher, seeking to divide and set apart—the dissonance is obvious.

This is why understanding immigration cannot be reduced to numbers, economics, or good intentions. It is about whether newcomers share in these instincts—whether their own values harmonise with Britain's soundtrack or jar against it. Private diversity enriches; public dissonance unsettles.

So here we stand. Britain's past explains its present character. Its present character will decide its future. The question now is simple: when people come to Britain from every corner of the globe, how do they experience these values?

Some groups blend in so well they appear more British than the British themselves. Others? Their alignment is patchier—and it shows. Finally, for a significant number, their values are well-aligned with their countries of origin as a matter of survival. But living according to the British values we have defined is a massive stretch, incredibly difficult, seemingly impossible.

> *If I found it somewhat difficult emigrating from a culture steeped in British values, but not being British. It must be utterly daunting for those with fundamentally different rules for the way life is lived.*

So what happens to non-Britons when they find themselves on these shores: firstly, there are those who fit like a missing puzzle piece, secondly those who may integrate over a generation or two, and finally those who, with no intended malice, risk friction and misery for both themselves and the British.

That is the task of the next part of our story.

7 Can You Join the Queue?
How Non-Britons Adapt—or Don't

The Challenge

So here we stand. The values are not abstract slogans, but living habits, passed down like an heirloom teapot. They are the prism through which we can understand those who may be naturally comfortable with entirely different values.

All of this raises a pressing question. Can Britain's distinctive values survive mass immigration from cultures that do not share some or all of them? What about even small numbers of people whose long term survival has forged diametrically opposed values? What is the impact on Britons who have worked doggedly for centuries to create them?

Many immigrant groups embrace British habits eagerly. But some arrive with values developed to survive and thrive in environments and circumstances very different to Britain. It is understandably difficult to adapt. The same would be for the "average Briton" to emigrate and live in their country. Imagine that?

I noted above that even though the values of my upbringing were very close to British values, South African values are different. In South Africa, we have a different sense of personal space. We kiss everyone hello, or used to. As kids going to play at a friend's house, we would always kiss their mother hello and goodbye and call her "Aunty (first name)" never, Mrs so-and-so. This is not a thing in Britain. When my parents visited the UK in 1962, my mother was kissing everyone hello, not noticing how uncomfortable our relatives were. It took a frank cousin to tell my father to tell her to stop.

My first year in Britain reminded me of my first year at boarding school—overwhelmed, feeling at times I was being bullied when it was just the way the British offered me a chance to "join in". Finding a bridge to British culture through one or two values first seemed to work. Now, after 30 years, I feel alien in South Africa.

When people keep separate, it really jars with Britain's legacy. Tolerance only works when the core values are shared. Normans, Celts, Saxons—all bent, adapted, and became part of Britain. Immigrants may thrive more if they did the same. They are in Britain. They owe this to the Britons. And to themselves. Fairness, individual rights, joining in, keeping calm—for Britons these are not negotiable. They are the essence of Britain.

The Norman Test Case

The Normans arrived as conquerors in 1066, speaking French and despising the locals. Who would have thought. Within a century, they were "English". Their language fused with Anglo-Saxon, and their barons were bound by Magna Carta. Every wave of newcomers was eventually absorbed—but only by adapting to the island's rules. The test today is the same.

Integration Today

The challenge is clear. Fundamentally, newcomers from clan-based societies often bring values that clash with Britain's. If tribal loyalty trumps individual rights then British values are not just ignored but undermined. For the British, it is a case of "been there, done that", finished with that 300 years ago.

When the Scots rose to restore Bonnie Prince Charlie—the Catholic grandson of the deposed James II—to the English throne, they weren't simply backing a lost cause for romance's sake. Many Highland clans saw it as a chance to return the rightful Stuart line to power and to reclaim their own influence under a king who shared their faith and clan-based system. The English, watching this rebellion unfold, drew a lasting conclusion: a Scot's loyalty to clan and cause would always outweigh loyalty to crown. Their solution was blunt— ban the clans, kilts, pipes, and broadswords for decades. Tartan itself were a seditious pamphlet.

> *My great, great, great grandmother, Isabella Fraser (nee MacTavish) was one of the first women to marry in tartan in 1785 shortly after wearing tartan became legal again. Her famous Fraser tartan wedding dress is on display at the Inverness Museum and Art Gallery. It is the only known surviving 18th-century women's tartan gown and has been passed down through our family for generations. My father's cousin wore it on a parade through Inverness at the end of the Second World War.*

Then there was the case of sectarian violence. After a century of Catholics and Protestants trying to bludgeon each other into holiness, Britain decided the game wasn't worth it. The compromise was classic: keep your Mass, keep your Bible, but for heaven's sake keep it down—because nothing spoils Sunday lunch like religious conflict. That was 400 years ago.

Britain's history shows that integration requires adaptation. Normans, Celts, Scots—all bent into a shared culture. The same must be asked today.

A Patchwork, Not a Single Cloth

Britons often talk about "immigrants" as though they were a single group. The truth is that immigration since the 1950s isn't one story, but many, stitched together into a patchwork quilt. Immigrants are incredibly diverse and understandably have wildly differing values. The British are not.

Some readers may be interested in the numbers, and the main geographic origins and locations in Britain of immigrants. Also, the main eras of immigration and reasons for this. This information is based on historical and demographic research from the UK Parliament Library, the Office of National Statistics, Migration Observatory (Oxford), and BBC archives. In order of the most to least populous:

Major Non-Briton Communities in the UK

1. Pakistanis (~1.6 million)

- **Main Migration Periods / Reasons:** 1950s–1970s (post-war labour recruitment); 1970s–2000s (family reunification).
- **Areas of Origin:** Azad Kashmir, Punjab, Karachi (Mirpuri heritage dominant in West Yorkshire).
- **Key UK Settlements:** Birmingham, Bradford, Manchester, East London.

2. Hindus (~1 million)

- **Main Migration Periods / Reasons:** 1960s–1970s (professional migration), East African expulsions (Uganda, Kenya, Tanzania); continuing arrivals from India for education and business.
- **Areas of Origin:** Gujarat, Maharashtra, Punjab, Bengal, East Africa.
- **Key UK Settlements:** Leicester, Harrow, Wembley, Birmingham (Neasden Temple globally known).

3. Poles (~740 000)

- **Main Migration Periods / Reasons:** Post-war 1940s (Polish servicemen and refugees); 2004–2016 mainly (EU free movement for work).
- **Areas of Origin:** Warsaw, Kraków, Gdańsk, Wrocław.
- **Key UK Settlements:** London, Birmingham, Manchester, Slough (dense Polish-Catholic parishes).

4. Bangladeshis (~700 000)

- **Main Migration Periods / Reasons:** 1950s–1970s (industrial labour: textiles, catering; later family reunification).
- **Areas of Origin:** Sylhet District (North-East Bangladesh).

- **Key UK Settlements:** Tower Hamlets (Brick Lane), Birmingham, Oldham.

5. Caribbean / West Indians (~600,000, with larger second- and third-generation descendants)

- **Main Migration Periods / Reasons**: 1948–1973 (invited from British colonies and Commonwealth territories to help rebuild post-war Britain, especially in transport, healthcare, and industry. The Empire Windrush ship arrived in 1948, giving the generation its name.)
- **Areas of Origin**: Jamaica, Trinidad & Tobago, Barbados, Grenada, St Lucia, St Vincent, Antigua.
- **Key UK Settlements**: London (Brixton, Notting Hill, Tottenham), Birmingham, Bristol, Leeds, Manchester.

6. Romanians (~550 000)

- **Main Migration Periods / Reasons:** 1990s (post-Communist emigration); 2007 onwards (EU accession enabling work migration).
- **Areas of Origin:** Transylvania, Moldavia, Wallachia.
- **Key UK Settlements:** London, Luton, Birmingham.

7. Sikhs (~520 000)

- **Main Migration Periods / Reasons:** 1950s–1970s (industrial labour migration and Kenya-Uganda expellees. Peak 1960s Midlands industrial expansion, 1970s onwards (family reunification.)
- **Areas of Origin:** Punjab (India).
- **Key UK Settlements:** Southall, Birmingham, Leicester, Wolverhampton (notable Gurdwara Sri Guru Singh Sabha).

8. Chinese (~400 000)

- **Main Migration Periods / Reasons:** 1950s–1980s (Hong Kong seafarers, restaurant trade); 2000s onwards (students and professionals from mainland China).
- **Areas of Origin:** Hong Kong, Guangdong, Beijing, Shanghai.
- **Key UK Settlements:** London (Chinatown), Manchester, Liverpool.

9. Mediterranean Europeans (~400 000)

- **Main Migration Periods / Reasons:** 1950s–present (post-war reconstruction, catering, academia).
- **Areas of Origin:** Italy (Lazio, Sicily), Greece (Cyprus), Spain, Portugal.
- **Key UK Settlements:** London, Bedford (Italian Lazio), Birmingham, North London (Cypriot communities).

10. Arabs (~400 000)

- **Main Migration Periods / Reasons:** 1950s–1970s (Yemeni seamen); 1980s–2000s (refugees from Iraq, Syria, Lebanon; students and investors from Gulf states.)
- **Areas of Origin:** Yemen, Iraq, Egypt, Syria, Lebanon, Gulf region.
- **Key UK Settlements:** London (Edgware Road), Birmingham.

11. Central Europeans (~350 000)

- **Main Migration Periods / Reasons:** 2004 EU enlargement; education and hospitality sectors.
- **Areas of Origin:** Czech Republic, Slovakia, Hungary.
- **Key UK Settlements:** London, Manchester.

12. Other EU Europeans (~300 000)

- **Main Migration Periods / Reasons:** 1990s–present (corporate, academic and service sectors).
- **Areas of Origin:** Netherlands, Belgium, Scandinavia, Austria.
- **Key UK Settlements:** London, Edinburgh, Oxford, Cambridge.

13. Ex-Yugoslavs & Albanians (~250 000)

- **Main Migration Periods / Reasons:** 1990s (Balkan wars); 2000s (economic migration).
- **Areas of Origin:** Kosovo, Albania, Bosnia, Croatia, Serbia, North Macedonia.
- **Key UK Settlements:** London, Birmingham, Manchester (Albanians concentrated in East London).

14. South Africans (~220 000)

- **Main Migration Periods / Reasons:** 1990s–present (post-apartheid skilled migration and dual citizens).
- **Areas of Origin:** Johannesburg, Cape Town, Durban.
- **Key UK Settlements:** London, Surrey, Berkshire.

15. Nigerians (~215 000)

- **Main Migration Periods / Reasons:** 1980s–1990s (students, professionals and political exiles. Later: healthcare and finance.)
- **Areas of Origin:** Yoruba, Igbo, Hausa-Fulani regions.
- **Key UK Settlements:** London (Peckham = "Little Lagos"), Manchester, Birmingham.

16. Filipinos (~200 000)

- **Main Migration Periods / Reasons:** 1990s–2010s (NHS and care sector employment).
- **Areas of Origin:** Luzon, Visayas.
- **Key UK Settlements:** London, Manchester, Birmingham.

17. Americans (~160 000)

- **Main Migration Periods / Reasons:** Ongoing since post-war 1940 (finance, media, diplomatic and academic roles).
- **Areas of Origin:** New York, California, Midwest.
- **Key UK Settlements:** London, Oxford, Cambridge.

18. South-East Asians (~150 000)

- **Main Migration Periods / Reasons:** 1970s–1980s (Vietnamese "boat people"); 2000s (Thai, Malaysian and Indonesian workers and students).
- **Areas of Origin:** Vietnam, Thailand, Malaysia, Indonesia.
- **Key UK Settlements:** London, Birmingham, university towns.

19. Sri Lankans (~130 000)

- **Main Migration Periods / Reasons:** 1980s–1990s (Tamil civil war refugees and economic migration).
- **Areas of Origin:** Jaffna (Tamils), Colombo (Sinhalese).
- **Key UK Settlements:** Harrow, Croydon, Wembley.

20. Somalis (~120 000)

- **Main Migration Periods / Reasons:** 1980s–1990s (civil war refugees); 2000s: family reunification.
- **Areas of Origin:** Mogadishu, Hargeisa.
- **Key UK Settlements:** London (Camden, Tower Hamlets), Birmingham, Leicester, Cardiff.

21. Australians (~120 000)

- **Main Migration Periods / Reasons:** 1950s–present (Commonwealth links, work visas, heritage ties).
- **Areas of Origin:** Sydney, Melbourne, Perth.
- **Key UK Settlements:** London (Earl's Court = "Kangaroo Valley"), Bristol.

22. Iranians (~90 000)

- **Main Migration Periods / Reasons:** Post-1979 (Revolution exiles; ongoing students and business migration).
- **Areas of Origin:** Tehran, Shiraz, Isfahan.
- **Key UK Settlements:** London (Kensington "Tehrangeles"), Manchester.

23. Canadians (~90 000)

- **Main Migration Periods / Reasons:** 1950s–present (academic, media, and corporate sectors).
- **Areas of Origin:** Toronto, Vancouver, Montreal.
- **Key UK Settlements:** London, Edinburgh.

24. Afghans (~80 000)

- **Main Migration Periods / Reasons:** 1980s–1990s (Soviet war refugees); 2001–present (Taliban conflict and asylum seekers).
- **Areas of Origin:** Kabul, Herat, Kandahar.
- **Key UK Settlements:** West London (Hounslow, Southall), Birmingham.

25. Russians (~70 000)

- **Main Migration Periods / Reasons:** 1990s post-Soviet financial elite migration; 2000s investors, students and political exiles.

- **Areas of Origin:** Moscow, St Petersburg, Caucasus.
- **Key UK Settlements:** London (Kensington "Londongrad"), Surrey.

26. New Zealanders (~60 000)

- **Main Migration Periods / Reasons:** 1950s–present (Commonwealth ties and professional migration).
- **Areas of Origin:** Auckland, Wellington, Christchurch.
- **Key UK Settlements:** London (Clapham rugby circle), Manchester.

27. Eritreans (~28 000)

- **Main Migration Periods / Reasons:** 1990s–2000s (refugees from conflict and conscription).
- **Areas of Origin:** Nationwide across Eritrea.
- **Key UK Settlements:** London (Brixton, Stockwell), Leeds, Birmingham, Glasgow.

Finding the Rhythm: How Newcomers Move with Britain's Tune

Immigration is often measured in numbers: how many arrived, how many left, how many pounds they cost or contribute. Politicians juggle figures as though Britain were a ledger. But numbers miss the point.

Immigration is also never as simple as "they fit" or "they don't". If only life were like a jigsaw puzzle, where every new piece clicks neatly into place. In Britain, it's more like inviting newcomers to join a pub quiz team. Some arrive already humming the theme from *Mastermind*, delighted to join in and even better at the picture round than the locals. Others prefer to huddle at their own table, comparing answers quietly in a language nobody else speaks. And a few wander into the pub, look suspiciously at the quizmaster, and ask why anyone should bother answering questions in the first place.

The truth is, how non-Britons settle depends less on passports and paperwork and more on how naturally they stride, stumble or bump into Britain's values: fairness that insists on equal treatment, suspicion of anyone too full of themselves, joining in with a smile, cheerfulness in the drizzle, and a fondness for tinkering rather than toppling. Some pick it up like second nature. Some take a generation or two. And some never quite stop looking at the locals as though they were rude to their leaders, disloyal to their families, wasting their time on strangers, or slightly mad.

Why Values Are So Hard to Change

Changing a person's values isn't like changing your socks—it's more like changing your bones. Psychologists such as Milton Rokeach (*The Nature of Human Values*, 1973) and social scientists like Shalom Schwartz (*Basic Human Values Theory*, 1992) show that values sit at the deepest level of identity—below opinions, below habits, below politics. They are absorbed early, reinforced daily, and defended instinctively. It's why a Londoner and a Liverpudlian will argue furiously about football, yet both recoil in unison when someone jumps a queue.

Moral cognition researchers conclude that your brain doesn't like it when you rethink your values; it hits the panic button as if you've just seen a lion, not a moral dilemma. In short, our sense of "right" and "fair" is welded to emotion, not reason. Differences in values can make us more angry and upset in ways that other differences never do. It's what makes cultural integration so tricky: you can adopt the accent but rewiring what feels fair or decent may take generations, if ever. The pain from differences in values starts between Britons and non-Britons and ends between different generations within non-Britons. No-one has a free ride.

Those Who've Fitted In with Grace

Some newcomers arrive and seem to breathe in the air of Britain as if they've always known its weather. They may not know all the verses of *God Save the King*, but then most Britons don't either! In fairness, the number of verses has varied significantly over time. But they understand instinctively when to murmur "sorry" to a lamppost or when to form an orderly line without instruction. Their approach to belonging is understated: they don't demand a seat at the table, they quietly bring a seat and offer to pour tea.

They grasp that *fairness* is Britain's unofficial religion—that the same rules for everyone are the glue holding together a nation otherwise famous for disagreeing about everything. Fair play means the referee's whistle applies to everyone, whether you're a duke or a dustman. Ignore that, and you don't just risk disapproval. You risk the collective chill of a nation that believes it is better to lose than to win by bending the rules.

You can see it at the bus stop. Non-Britons who fit in stand in quiet, invisible order, each one knowing exactly who was there first. Try to cut in, and the silence tightens—a few coughs, a shuffle of feet, and a raised eyebrow.

Individuality is the crown jewel of British life: each person stands as themselves, not as a cousin, clan member, or collective echo. Some outsiders resonate instantly. They debate with fire, publish boldly, and argue without flinching. They are, in essence, free individuals—and Britain warms to them.

Some newcomers are instinctually suspicious of power. They question leaders, satirise authority, and argue their own side with relish. Britons clap quietly in approval. This scepticism aligns with the British instinct to distrust anyone "too big for their boots".

Some outsiders excel at making an effort to belong. Some build beautiful temples and others their churches, yes. But they also sit on the Parent Teachers Association and run the local Post Office or corner shop. Their heritage stays intact, but their faces shine in the wider crowd. They enter politics to represent everyone in their constituency not just fellow immigrants from the same country. They make a visible effort. Britain notices this, and it approves.

Britain admires those who serve. Soldiers, nurses, volunteers— they are heroes. Outsiders who share this instinct win deep respect. Gurkhas are beloved for their loyalty. Sikhs are honoured for their tradition of selfless service. They prove duty is universal.

When all else fails, Britain jokes. Train cancelled? Laugh. Apocalypse tomorrow? Make tea, then laugh. Outsiders who share this instinct bond instantly. The Irish black humour and laughter at funerals are natural cousins here. The resilience of well-aligned non-Britons who laugh even in grief and joke in despair feels like home.

These groups have kept their heritage intact while blending seamlessly into the national rhythm—like new instruments joining an old orchestra, their accents may differ, but they play beautifully in tune. Britain notices and quietly approves.

Those Still Finding Their Footing

Others walk the same streets but to a slightly different rhythm. They respect the law, but not necessarily *the spirit* of it—where Britain sees a level playing field, they see a game to be negotiated. They cherish family and faith deeply, but sometimes so tightly that they leave little room for the wider circle of community. They mean no harm; they simply arrive from worlds where kinship is protection, hierarchy is security, and compromise can seem like weakness. To those raised in a culture of connections, it feels natural, even kind. Giving preference to family and clan is as natural as breathing. But to Britons, who believe even billionaires should wait their turn, it is unthinkable.

Their instinct is to speak together, to gather in groups, to speak as one voice. In their minds, speaking loudly is sincerity, but to British ears it sounds like theatre. Where the Briton prefers a raised eyebrow and a murmured complaint, they may prefer a megaphone and a crowd. To them, it's strength. To Britons, it feels like individuality drowned in chaos and mob rule.

For them, the instinct to defer to authority still runs deep, and the idea that even a monarch must face public heckling can take years to digest. Their sense of *duty* is often powerful—but directed first to family, then faith, then local community and only lastly to the public good. Leaders are greeted with deference, titles, ceremony. It's not servility, but to British eyes it comes close. What is a threat to British life are leaders who are easily able to marshal the minds of non-Britons to one purpose against the interests of Britons. The British look askance: "But who's keeping them in check?"

Some newcomers keep within their circles. They shop in their own markets, eat their own food, and live their own lives politely apart. It isn't hostility, but neither is it reaching out. The promise is left half-kept. To Britons, it feels like someone dipping a toe in the pool but never swimming.

Admitting an error is seen as weakness and disloyalty to the family or clan. Admissions are therefore partial, excuses slip in, half-hearted corrections take time.

Hardship happens to us all. Britons make a joke about it. Others can take hardship melodramatically and may feel deliberately targeted by the majority, are quickly offended, rather than seeing it as bad luck or fate. Wailing, shouting, theatrical protest? Moving, yes, but draining. A joke would ease the weight.

And when it comes to change, Britons believe in hours of debate and consultation. Others prefer noise. Demonstrations, graffiti, chanting in streets, marches, slogans, shouted demands. It shows passion, but to British eyes it feels melodramatic. They wonder why the same energy isn't spent writing a petition.

Integration for them is a difficult process of letting go. Many are working it out, balancing inherited customs with British expectations of politeness, self-deprecation, and participation. They are caught in a values "no man's land". They may be praised for their industry and then doubted for their insularity. It takes years to learn that a small change in tone can make all the difference between suspicion and acceptance.

Those Struggling Most to Find Common Ground

And then there are those for whom British life feels almost alien. They come from lands where authority is absolute, where dissent is dangerous, and where *order* is kept not by consent but by fear. There, a joke about the ruler can mean exile with a bounty on your head. In Britain, the same joke wins a BAFTA.

To them, Britain's endless debates look like chaos, and its politeness a form of weakness or stupidity. They may admire freedom in theory but mistrust it in practice—freedom of speech sounds reckless, *humour in hardship* disrespectful or asinine, and gradual reform suspiciously slow.

Their worlds were built on *obedience*, not questioning, on *loyalty to kin*, not fairness to strangers. So, when they meet Britain's invisible moral scaffolding—equality before the law, queuing, self-deprecating humour, admitting mistakes out loud—they sometimes freeze. It is not hostility that keeps them apart, but unfamiliarity with a system that expects individuals to think for themselves, justify their moral choices and to laugh at themselves too.

The most difficult case is when communities stay entirely apart—avoiding smiles, dodging difficult conversations, never joining in. Britain prizes the smile in the shop, the eyebrow raised in mockery. The British expect reciprocity. If the promise isn't answered with effort, they see it not as people wanting their privacy to live separate lives, but as rejection. As if British culture is inferior. Harder to change still are habits that obscure individuality entirely and muffle voices.

It's the same instinct that makes neighbours nod when they pass. The gesture is small, but its absence is glaring. Without those signals, social life feels like a door closed in your face. They remember when Covid masks turned every trip to the shops into a low-stakes farce, where neighbours failed to recognise each other, waved uncertainly at strangers, and discovered just how psychologically disturbing it is to have your own face classified as "password not accepted".

And then there are behaviours that jar altogether: groups muscling into spaces, graffiti marking territory, scowls at strangers or sectarian politics. Britain has tasted deathly sectarian politics twice before and found it as appetising as cold vomit.

Where duty is only to family, or clan, Britain bristles. Service earns honour here. Taking without giving to the public earns quiet contempt. Nothing annoys quite like someone thinking social welfare is something they deserve merely by their existence and Britain is rich enough anyway. Headline: Britain is borrowing unsustainably just to survive.

And where there is no humour at all—only silence, grim anger, or public scowling—Britain feels alien. For Britons, laughter is not denial. It is survival. Without humour, even the weather would have beaten them centuries ago. Humour doesn't erase pain; it makes it bearable.

As they naturally retreat into enclaves, where familiar rules prevail and suspicion of the host culture grows, the situation spirals downwards. The tragedy is not that they cannot integrate, however difficult it is, but that no one has explained that the entrance exam is social, not bureaucratic.

Closing Reflection

All of this, psychologists remind us, is predictable. Values are not opinions to be updated like phone software; they are deep mental grooves, carved by centuries of survival. Jonathan Haidt's work on moral foundations shows that societies develop different moral "taste buds" depending on what kept them alive—some prize loyalty, others fairness; some worship order, others liberty. Asking someone to swap one set for another is like asking a pianist to play violin overnight.

In the end, values are not lofty words. They live in how people behave in public: whether they smile at strangers or scowl, whether they keep noise down or shout across buses, whether they join the fête or stick inside their bubble. Do they pick up after themselves or scrawl their marks on the wall?

Some newcomers seem born to Britain's way. Others hover in polite half-steps. And some habits clash so badly that muttering begins. But Britain's values are not locked to non-Britons. They are open to anyone who tries—who plays fair, joins in, serves others, owns mistakes, and laughs in the rain.

Britain welcomes many ways of living, but its values have a grain. Those who rub along with it find belonging. Those who saw across it make splinters. In the next chapter, we celebrate those who have captured Britain's heart and, in doing so, reminded Britons of their own.

8 How Outsiders Win Britain's Heart

From Nadiya's Bake-Off Smile to Mo Farah's Finish Line

Those who embrace British values—immigrants, their children, even the occasional celebrity who stumbled across the Channel or the Pond—find that Britain embraces them back. Those who reject them? They often discover that British affection, once lost, is hard to win again.

So, let's meet some who made it. And one or two who didn't.

Nadiya Hussain

Born in Luton to Bangladeshi parents, Nadiya grew up in a close-knit community where ambition for women often meant quiet domesticity. She found escape in baking—therapy for her anxiety, a way of creating joy amid struggle.

Then came *The Great British Bake Off*. Week after week, her warmth, tears, and gentle humour made her a household name. When her cakes collapsed, she laughed. When she won, she gave a speech so heartfelt that Britain melted: "I'm never going to put boundaries on myself ever again."

The free individual had claimed her space. *Joining In the British Way* had been fulfilled, not with a crown or medal, but with a Victoria sponge. She showed that contribution, honesty, and laughter are the ingredients Britain values most.

Mo Farah

Born in Mogadishu, Somalia, Mo arrived in Britain as a child refugee. His start was harsh: civil war, displacement, a new language, a new life in Hounslow. Yet instead of bitterness, Mo found running shoes. He ran, and kept running, until he became the poster boy for London 2012.

On "Super Saturday", as he sprinted to Olympic gold in the 10,000 metres, the roar of the stadium seemed to carry him forward. The Union Jack draped over his shoulders, his "Mobot" celebration on live TV—it wasn't just sport, it was national catharsis. Here was a refugee child, now Britain's champion.

What made him beloved wasn't just medals. It was the humility, the grin, the willingness to laugh at himself in interviews. That was *duty before self, fair play*, and *humour in hardship* in one body. Mo made Britain cry, not because he ran fast, but because he made them feel proud of what their country could be.

Malala Yousafzai

Born in Pakistan's Swat Valley, Malala nearly died for saying girls should learn. A Taliban bullet silenced her voice—briefly. Then Britain gave her treatment, safety, and schooling.

At Oxford, she studied like any other student, making jokes about hall food. On world stages, she spoke with calm, modest authority. She didn't rage; she smiled. That was *pushing boundaries* with grace.

Her presence in Britain became symbolic: proof that even in an age of cynicism, courage and humility could still move nations. Malala showed Britons that *the free individual* could be stronger than armies.

Gino D'Acampo

The Italian chef who first charmed *This Morning* viewers with unapologetically Mediterranean pasta has since become a caricature of cheerful integration. His self-deprecating humour, playful slips of the tongue, and knack for laughing at himself made him a daytime TV staple.

By leaning into his origins with warmth and wit, he captured a British instinct: turning embarrassment into comedy. The result is affection—he's now "our Gino", folded into national culture like the eccentric uncle who livens up Sunday lunch.

Fred Sirieix

Fred Sirieix, the French maître d' of *First Dates*, embodies professionalism with charm. Though unmistakably French, his fairness and warmth resonate with British audiences. He champions courtesy without pomp, turning hospitality into theatre.

By poking gentle fun at his Frenchness against British awkwardness, he absorbed a local habit of laughing with, not at, differences. The response has been warm: Fred is no longer "the French maître d'", but simply Fred, a trusted guide who models civility and decency.

Prue Leith

Prue Leith, born in South Africa, slid so smoothly into Britain's national life that few remember she wasn't raised here. She built her reputation as a chef, restaurateur, and writer, but her real cultural breakthrough came with *The Great British Bake Off*. Her crisp judgments, eccentric spectacles, and blend of firmness with warmth made her instantly recognisable.

In many ways, she embodies the British balance of seriousness with humour: she delivers criticism, but with twinkling kindness, never cruelty. The public reaction has been warmth—she is seen less as "the South African-born judge" and more as the wise aunt of

British television, proof that belonging often comes with tone and temperament rather than birthplace.

Mohamed Salah

Born in Nagrig, Egypt, Salah arrived in Liverpool with little English and less fanfare. Yet in a city that values humility and humour, he fitted in perfectly.

He scored goals by the dozen, but what endeared him was his character. He did the school run like any other dad. He missed penalties with sheepish shrugs, not tantrums.

Liverpool fans sing his name, but what they really love is his embodiment of *fair play*, *humour in hardship*, and *duty before self*. Mo Salah became proof that even global superstars could be grounded Scousers at heart.

Zadie Smith

Born in Willesden to a Jamaican mother and an English father, Zadie grew up surrounded by different cultures. She turned it into art.

Her debut novel, *White Teeth* (2000), was a sensation: funny, sprawling, and full of characters stumbling through multicultural London. It wasn't a lecture; it was a laugh, a mirror, a celebration.

Her humour is sharp, her prose elegant, but what makes her beloved is her free individuality. She is unapologetically mixed, unapologetically London, unapologetically herself. By telling immigrant stories with wit and dignity, she reflected Britain back to itself—contradictions and all.

Ruby Wax

Ruby Wax: American by passport but long since absorbed into Britain's cultural bloodstream, made her name by dismantling the pompous with a laugh. Her comedy was brash by British standards, but she bent it into self-deprecation, turning her own neuroses into a kind of cultural currency.

Later, as a mental health campaigner, she embodied a distinctly British way of dealing with difficulty: honesty shot through with humour.

Sir Trevor McDonald

Born in Trinidad, Trevor came to Britain with a voice like velvet and a presence like granite. On ITV News, he delivered wars, scandals, and elections with calm authority.

What made him trusted was not drama, but dignity. He embodied *suspicion of power*—delivering facts without spin—and *fair play*, treating every story with seriousness.

He became more than a newsreader. He became the nation's voice of conscience, the man Britons trusted when the world seemed uncertain. In living rooms across the land: Trevor wasn't an immigrant anymore, he was family.

Dame Zaha Hadid

Born in Baghdad, Zaha arrived in Britain with visions too big for her time. For years, critics dismissed her designs as fanciful sketches. She refused to give in.

But her buildings became world icons:

- The London Aquatics Centre for the 2012 Olympics—a wave of steel and glass over the pools.
- The MAXXI Museum in Rome—concrete ribbons frozen mid-flow.
- The Guangzhou Opera House—twin glass "pebbles", vast and organic.
- The Heydar Aliyev Center in Baku—a swooping cultural hub, almost alive in its curves.

Her brilliance was pure British eccentricity: *pushing boundaries*, refusing compromise, and eventually bending the skyline itself. When she died, Britain mourned not just an architect, but a woman who proved outsiders could redraw the map of the world.

Princess Diana vs. Meghan Markle (The Duchess of Sussex, Countess of Dumbarton and Baroness Kilkeel): Two Paths

The British monarchy has always been a mirror for the nation's values. Some royals have reflected them back in ways that stirred admiration at home and abroad. Others, despite opportunities and goodwill, seemed to miss the rhythm of what makes Britain tick. Few comparisons show this contrast more starkly than Princess Diana and Meghan Markle. Both were women who married into the royal family under a spotlight brighter than any stage. Both faced relentless scrutiny. Yet the ways they responded could not have been more different—one turning adversity into affection, the other seemed to see scrutiny as hostility.

I think about my own experiences when thinking about Meghan. I mentioned that moving to Britain felt like my first year in boarding school. The hilarious 1986 *Spitting Image* hit "I've never met a nice South African" was still on people's lips and was often sung mockingly in my face—proof that cultural welcomes in Britain can be tough. It can be like that.

I think I gave the impression to some that I was "too big for my boots" and they played with my ego like a group of friends playfully throwing around a tennis ball. I soon realised that this was their way of saying that they liked me, but that I needed to temper my overt confidence, important as a front in South Africa but off-putting in Britain, before they would offer me an invitation to the garden party and later to the dinner party. I often think about this when I consider the fate of Meghan Markle.

Princess Diana

As a Briton, Diana instinctively understood Britain's values more than most and lived them publicly. She shook hands with AIDS patients at a time when fear and stigma silenced others—an act of *simple fairness* and humanity that broke barriers not just in Britain, but worldwide. She walked through minefields in Angola, not for theatre, but to give voice to the voiceless, embodying *duty before self* in a way that even the toughest cynics found moving. She leavened pain with *humour in hardship*—shy smiles, self-deprecating quips, and the grace to laugh at her own missteps. She embraced the notion that she may be made fun of since she had position and privilege. She joined in the public square like no royal had done before or done since: seeking to shake everyone's hand in those first years whenever she and Prince Charles appeared in public. To the British public, she wasn't flawless, but she was recognisably human, and recognisably intensely British in her way of being. They were proud of her since she mirrored British values as they instinctively understood them. That is why she became the "People's Princess", loved not only at home but across continents, and why her untimely death was mourned with a depth of feeling rarely seen in modern history.

Meghan Markle, Duchess of Sussex

Meghan faced the same furnace of attention, but the values she grew up with took her in another direction. Where Diana saw the press as a tool—however flawed—for causes larger than herself, Meghan appeared to see it as an adversary. Where Diana, understanding the British value of pulling down those who got too big for their boots, met criticism with warmth, even humour, Meghan seemed to react with hurt. That type of press treatment in America might signal the end of a celebrity's career—a disaster. In Britain, it was a day at the office. Where Diana transformed sometimes adverse scrutiny into strength, Meghan was understandably alarmed and troubled by it. Rather than leaning into the British way of disarming tension with a joke at her expense, she withdrew, seeming to me to frame herself as a victim of forces she could never control because to her they were so alien. The affection that greeted her entry into royal life quietly slipped away, her popularity falling as quickly as it had once risen.

The Lesson

Diana turned Britain's values into a universal language—*fair play, duty before self, humour in hardship, joining in*—and the world adored her for it. For Meghan those values or the way some of them are played out culturally were unfamiliar. She withdrew seemingly wounded, and Britain, in turn, withdrew its affection. The contrast is not just about personality; it is about the deep current of British values that, when embraced, lift individuals to heights of love and respect, and when misunderstood, leave them adrift. The choice between the two paths is still open to anyone who wishes to belong, including Meghan, who would be loved even more for having walked away but then returning to embrace British values.

But while Britain cheers on those who align with its values, the cracks keep widening underfoot for Britons themselves. Flags and smiles can't disguise the truth: a country that once led the world is now tripping over its own shoelaces. And so the question shifts—not who has joined us or kept separate, but what happens when we forget our values.

9 At War With Ourselves
Britain Without Its Values

Britain is like a fine oak table. Its grain runs deep: *Fair Play for All*, The *Free Individual, Suspicion of Power, Joining In the British Way, Owning Our Mistakes, Duty Before Self, Humour in Hardship, Evolution Not Revolution*, and *Pushing Boundaries*. Go with the grain and the surface gleams. Saw across it, and it protests in splinters.

Politicians, from Tony Blair to David Cameron and Rishi Sunak, have tried sawing their own way. Some polish, some varnish, some slap on paint. Yet the grain remains. And whenever governments go against it, Britain mutters that fateful verdict: "Not on".

This chapter holds up a mirror to today's Britain. The fights feel modern—immigration rows, NHS waiting lists, free speech spats, cost of living, crime—but their root is ancient: forgetting the values that once kept the nation steady. This isn't about left or right, Labour, Tory, the Greens, Reform, the Liberal Democrats and so on. It's about a nation that misplaced its own compass and was too polite (or too guilted) to insist on finding it again.

We were told our values were shameful, relics of empire, and we locked them away. In their place for many it seems we have imported a set of fashionable, often foreign, glittering ivory-tower ideals—equality charters, bureaucratic tick-boxes, international "norms" that appear to serve nobody but the well-connected who seem unaffected by what they recommend. What has followed is turmoil.

Healthcare

Take the NHS. People will wait patiently at Wimbledon for strawberries without complaint. But wait a year for chemotherapy or a hip replacement? That feels like betrayal. The refusal to admit the scale of the backlog—or the fact that Britain spends ten times more on the NHS in real terms than in 1948—violates *Owning Our Mistakes*. Waiting lists now top 7.6 million treatments, the highest in recorded history.

The UK spends around £180 billion a year on health, roughly 11% of GDP, yet satisfaction levels have plunged to the lowest since the 1980s. We don't need another slogan or necessarily more money thrown at the problem. We need honesty about what's jammed, which treatments work best, and where money is wasted. The cure is not mysterious; it's in plain sight but hidden under the political football that more closely resembles a hand grenade. The people who can influence and conduct the changes needed seem to have no clue where to start: the problem overwhelms them. So do their sacred cows—principles they cling to which have long since outlived their "sell by" date. The spirit to Push the Boundaries has been lost: what's left is managerial tinkering dressed up as strategy.

Immigration

Immigration is another fight that seems new but isn't. People can and do cheer Mo Farah or Nadiya Hussain, proof that Britain isn't inhospitable. But when waves arrive without telling the Britons what is going on, when rules look bent, when those who seem to make no effort to join in and then appear to be treated better than those who do, resentment builds. What is an asylum seeker? No-one knows anymore, so sympathies evaporate.

Legal net migration stood at over 700,000 last year, more than double the level at the Brexit vote. Add to that tens of thousands of irregular Channel crossings and you see why many people feel played. Politicians like to pretend it's a numbers issue, but it's about *Fair Play for All* and *Joining In the British Way*. People will happily welcome newcomers who muck in, *contribute more than they take out*, adapt, and respect the rules. And the government must be serious about building houses or getting out of the way of house builders. But when Britons see enclaves of non-Britons spending their time shouting at each other in the street while the local animal shelter struggles for volunteers, they know the promise has been broken.

Brexit

Suspicion of power is another British instinct that has been sorely tested. Brexit wasn't about more money for the NHS—everyone knew that was just a catchy sound bite; it was about telling unelected power that its writ stops at Dover. If the British nobles told King John to take a running jump, imagine what they would have said to Philip II Augustus, King of France at that time, had he tried to impose his rule on them? It's unthinkable.

And yet, after voting to leave, Britain found itself still tangled in the courts, and the machinery of unelected quangos. Ministers posture, but the public know the real levers are pulled by "experts", Public Sector mandarins, and judges who appear to many to be legislating from the bench. Many believe that the deep state or Blob, as some now openly call it, needs radical pruning back to size and re-taught that it serves the elected government—not the other way round. Otherwise *Suspicion of Power* will curdle into outright contempt.

Immigration

Covid is the case study in how not to live by British values. Lockdowns stretched from "just three weeks" into months. Rules shifted like sand. Ministers hid behind "the science", which turned out to be guesswork and groupthink. *Owning Our Mistakes* would have meant admitting that Covid wasn't uniform: deadly to some, a seasonal cold to the overwhelming majority of the population. The healthy were quarantined in a stunning reversal of public health logic. *Suspicion of Power* meant some people eventually stopped trusting the experts. And the refusal to publish lessons learned—or to explain why schools were closed while pubs reopened—still festers as a wound. The official inquiry, predicted to cost over £300 million—seemingly a plan drawn up by a low-talent bureaucrat or committee of the same—risks becoming yet another doorstop report filed under "too late".

The Economy

Economic policy is no better. Britain now borrows like a reckless heir, partying on the family silver and leaving the bill for the grandchildren. National debt has passed £2.7 trillion, roughly *100% of GDP*, the highest peacetime level since the 1960s. Services are strained, housing scarce, pensions shaky. This is generational theft dressed up as compassion. A Britain that once knew *Duty Before Self* now runs on "me first, someone else pays later". It's not sustainable.

Pension Pyramid Scheme

Perhaps national insurance has always been a Ponzi scheme with younger taxpayers paying for the pensions of retirees. With people living longer whilst birth rates decline, mass immigration is justified by an economic argument—more young workers from wherever they will come to fund pensions. And like all Ponzi schemes, it ends badly. After all, if your solution to being able to pay pensions is to keep importing more future pensioners, you've built a dangerous pyramid scheme, not an economy. Put another way, import one generation to pay for the last, then import a larger one to pay for them, and before long you need an arrivals hall the size of Yorkshire. And this is an understatement because this growth is exponential.

Education

Education is another case of fiddling while Rome burns. Britain once led the world with rigorous standards. Then came the bright ideas: "child-centred learning", coursework over exams, "everyone's a winner". International rankings plummeted, employers groaned, and some pupils left school unable to read or add up properly. In the most recent OECD PISA tests (the Program for International Student Assessment), British pupils ranked 13th in reading, 18th in maths, 13th in science—an embarrassment behind nations that spend far less and expect more. It took decades to admit the failure. This is the opposite of *Owning Our Mistakes*. While Finland and Singapore surged ahead with evidence-based teaching, Britain indulged in theories which should have stayed in "what if" seminars rather than unleashed on innocent children in classrooms.

Crime

And then there is crime. Nothing corrodes trust like the sense that law is not equal for all. A burglar can ransack your home, and the police may not even show up that day, or the next, or at all. Yet a clumsy tweet can summon officers to your door in hours on behalf of some mischievous outrage entrepreneur, performative complainer, undiagnosed narcissist or borderline personality disorder sufferer. This affects those on the political left and right.

Upside down standards shred *Fair Play for All*. Worse, the scandals of grooming gangs—covered up for fear of "community cohesion"—show what happens when *Owning Our Mistakes* is abandoned in favour of silence. Between 1997 and 2013, tens of thousands of children were abused while officials looked the other way. The cost is measured not just in headlines but in broken lives and a catastrophic loss of trust in the police.

Net Zero

Net Zero deserves its own entry in the hall of follies. Most Britons don't deny that stewardship of the planet matters. But when whatever Britain does will not move the needle, and the bills land on ordinary households first, suspicion turns into fury. Britain's tradition is *Evolution, Not Revolution*—gradual change, tested in committees backed by sound science and economics, rolled out carefully. Instead, we get grand targets and bans on this and that by what seems like virtue-signalling councillors, announced with fanfare. As if they've saved humanity. Household energy bills doubled between 2021 and 2023, largely thanks to global shocks but worsened by inflexible targets. If climate goals are ever to be met, they need to be developed and pursued the British way: hotly debated, practical, steady, and fair—not as if they were a religion with only one answer.

Free speech

Finally, perhaps most importantly, free speech, once a British export to the world, now limps at home. The world is aghast. Universities, meant to be arenas of argument, now resemble greenhouses: stifling, fragile, and overheated. Students learn quickly that one misstep brings outrage.

On social media, victimhood has become an Olympic sport. Everyone competes to be more aggrieved than the next. In this climate, *Humour in Hardship* withers. Instead of laughing at ourselves and the adverse situations we find ourselves in, either because of our own doing or fate, we point fingers at others. Instead of *Owning Our Mistakes*, we outsource blame to "the system". The result? A nation once famed for wit now risks drowning in sullen grievance.

Put all this together and the picture is clear. Today's fights—mass and illegal immigration, the NHS, debt, education, crime, climate, free speech—are not random. They are symptoms. Each time a value is ignored or violated, they will impact policy and the cracks spread wider.

The lesson is simple, almost embarrassingly so: reaffirm the British values—what is in and what is out—and get out of the way. For the most part, problems sort themselves out without massive intervention and money when the fundamental issues are fixed, and then politicians get out of the way. Ignore the values, and the problems fester, multiply, poison trust and bankrupt a nation. The cure isn't hidden. It has been developed by us for centuries. We just need the nerve—and perhaps the humour—to pick it up again.

Deep down, the fights are principally about leaders who are ignoring a nation's values to rather drive some other agenda that gets applause from cronies at home and friends abroad. Worse, citizens have been told that their values are wicked. They have been guilted into hiding them, and handed a stack of shiny substitutes that either collapse on contact with reality or melt in front of much harder-won British values that have stood the test of time. You can't run a country on buzzwords and box-ticking. Britain once ran half the world on common law and common sense; now it struggles to run a train on time.

Britain's cure lies in its own character—the instincts that once built liberty and fairness. To live by them again is urgent, not only for ourselves, but for a world still hungry for an example of courage and decency. Let us now consider the role Britain must once more claim on the world stage.

10 When Britain Remembers Who It Is

The Peculiar Island That Once Led the World—and Can Again

Leading the world isn't glamorous. It's lonely, messy, and full of mistakes. Gears grind, the brakes screech at times, but Britain never landed in a ditch or crashed into a tree. Britain at times stumbled, recalibrated, and carried on. It's not perfection—it's persistence—but the impact was huge.

Every civilisation has claimed to lead the way. Athens gave us democracy—or at least, democracy for land-owning men with beards. It was a glittering experiment, but fragile: two generations of brilliance followed by war, squabbling, and collapse. Still, the idea stuck: ordinary citizens could share power. But only about 10–15% of Athenians could vote. Women, slaves, foreigners, and anyone without the right pedigree were excluded. "Democracy" in Athens looked suspiciously like a gentlemen's debating club—brilliant, yes, but hardly universal.

Rome gave us law and empire. The Romans excelled at infrastructure development and order: roads, aqueducts, legions, statutes. They also excelled at conquest. But liberty was for Roman citizens, not for conquered provinces. Their gift was organisation, not freedom. Roman citizens enjoyed real legal protections: appeal to Caesar, property rights, due process. Everyone else? They were subjects, not citizens. The famous phrase *civis Romanus sum*—"I am a Roman citizen"—was less a declaration of pride than a get-out-of-jail-free card.

And don't forget the Jews. Alone among ancient peoples, they insisted that rulers themselves *must* answer to a higher law. Their prophets scolded kings and often paid for this with their lives Their scriptures enshrined justice, their God demanded accountability. This moral seed was immensely powerful and unique: the idea that law transcends power and everyone is born with rights that governments cannot create but need to protect.

So, by the Middle Ages, humanity had some tools: Israel's natural rights of the individual, Athens' flash of democracy and Rome's structure of law. But they were scattered, incomplete, and inconsistent. Liberty had been glimpsed but never secured.

These ideas would eventually find their most fertile soil not in the Papal States, the Holy Roman Empire, nor in the glamour of France—but in a damp, argumentative island right on the edge of the world.

Britons were never chosen in a divine sense. But by history's accidents and fusions—Celts, Saxons, Normans, and others forced to rub along—it became the nation that tested liberty in practice. Parliament, common law, habeas corpus, constitutional monarchy, abolition, universal voting, self-correction: Britain took humanity's scattered legacies and made them into habits, institutions, and exports.

Not that Britons were uniquely virtuous. They erred, sometimes badly. But unlike most, they persisted, owned-up to their mistakes, recalibrated, and pressed forward. Where others tore down, Britain tinkered. Where others imposed silence, Britain argued. Where others clung to empire until collapse, Britain built the Commonwealth.

This book tells that story: how Britain, more than any other nation, advanced a powerful constellation of values—fair play, liberty and individual dignity, suspicion of unchecked power, a promise of shared belonging, steady reform, duty beyond kin, honesty about mistakes, humour in hardship, and a restless urge to push boundaries.

These values are the true thread of Britain's tale. They shaped its scenery and its people, and they remain the key to whether Britain can flourish in the 21st century—when mass immigration, globalisation, and rival cultures test their strength.

If Athens lit the first torch, and Rome built the framework, and the Jews gave law its moral weight, it was Britain that carried liberty forward, step by stubborn step for a thousand years. Peculiar, muddling, never perfect—but leading humanity nonetheless.

Every civilisation has had to wrestle with the same question: how do you tame power without crushing liberty? How do you keep order without suffocating the people who must live under it? Most nations botched the exam. Britain, though far from perfect, sat in the front row and wrote out the first draft of the answers with lots of blotched ink, but the words were clear.

The French revolution spiralled into bloodshed too barbaric to mention. It was so severe that people begged for a strongman to restore order. Enter Napoleon, a general with a crown, turning "the people's revolution" into another monarchy, only with better uniforms. France learned—but it learned late.

Russia, a century later, toppled its Tsar only to replace him with something worse: Lenin, then Stalin, then the Gulag. A promised worker's paradise became an archipelago of labour camps. Millions perished. Where Britain had trial by jury, Russia had show trials. Where Britain had parliamentary opposition, Russia had purges. Liberty was a slogan, not a practice.

Germany and Italy stumbled into another ditch. Their experiments with parliamentary government gave way to street brawls, paramilitaries in matching shirts, and demagogues with clenched fists. The Brownshirts and Blackshirts promised national renewal but delivered catastrophe to the world. Again, the problem was the same: unchecked power, no culture of reform, no habit of compromise. Britain had endured Charles I and Oliver Cromwell, had clipped its monarchy with the Glorious Revolution, had cultivated suspicion of power. Germans and Italians were late to that lesson, and the world paid dearly.

Meanwhile across the Atlantic, America declared independence with lofty words borrowed almost wholesale from British pens. Jefferson from Locke. Madison from Montesquieu's observations of how Britain kept power in check. Montesquieu, the great French philosopher, studied English institutions during his three years in Britain, 1728 to 1731. He saw there a separation of powers in action, not in theory, and took it home in his *Spirit of the Laws.* The Founding Fathers designed a republic on the foundations of English common law, habeas corpus, and the balance of powers. America succeeded because it inherited Britain's homework.

And what of Britain's own children—Canada, Australia, New Zealand? These dominions were built on British institutions: parliaments, common law, jury trials, constitutional monarchy. They too wrestled with frontiers, diverse peoples, and the challenge of building liberty. But they did so with the British toolkit and so avoided the calamities of continental Europe.

Other ex-colonies tell a similar story. **India**, despite partition, is the world's largest democracy. **Pakistan**, for all its struggles, retains British legal structures and parliamentary forms. **Sri Lanka** and **Mauritius** took the same framework. **Botswana** has prospered with clean government since 1966. **Ghana, Kenya, and Nigeria**, though turbulent, maintain multiparty systems with elections that matter. **Barbados, Jamaica, Trinidad and Tobago, Belize, Cyprus, Malta**—all parliamentary democracies built on British blueprints. Some are tiny islands, but each demonstrates how institutions outlast empire.

Contrast this with the colonies of others. **French Indochina** (Vietnam, Laos, Cambodia) descended into war, dictatorship and mass murder in the case of Cambodia, their leaders all educated in the elite universities of Paris. **French Africa**—Mali, Chad, Niger, Central African Republic—became a carousel of coups. **Algeria's** independence was soaked in blood, its politics scarred ever since. **Belgium's Congo** was run as King Leopold's private estate, where millions died or were gratuitously mutilated for rubber quotas.

Portugal's Mozambique and Angola, run in the main by companies granted licenses, inherited only weak institutions and fell into decades of civil war, cruelty and Marxist misrule. **Brazil**, Portugal's great colony, passed through empire, oligarchy, and junta before stabilising late. But it sometimes feels as if Brazil treats the presidency like a roundabout: one term in office, the next in prison. Future leaders there don't just write their memoirs—they keep a toothbrush packed, just in case their "retirement home" comes with bars on the windows.

Dutch Indonesia spent its first decades in authoritarianism. **German colonies** in Africa were run with military brutality and left no lasting civic institutions. **Italian colonies** in Libya and East Africa were remembered for violence rather than governance.

And Britain's influence extended beyond empire. Even **Scandinavia**—often admired today as a model of prosperity and stability—took its cues in part from Britain. **Norway's** 1814 constitution, **Sweden's** 19th-century reforms, and **Denmark's** peaceful transition to constitutional monarchy all looked to Britain as the working example of *Evolution, Not Revolution.* **Finland**, when winning independence from Russia in 1917, deliberately borrowed from Westminster-style parliamentary traditions rather than its eastern neighbour's autocracy. The Nordic balance of liberty and duty is no coincidence: it chimes closely with the values Britain had been living out for centuries.

Other nations faced the same challenges as Britain but made different choices. Where Britain abolished slavery in 1833, America fought a civil war in the 1860s, and Brazil waited until 1888.

Where Britain extended the vote step by step, France swung between republic and empire, Russia between Tsar and commissar. Incidentally, France has always insisted it reveres women—it just took until 1944 to let them vote. For a country famed for romance, that's a rather long courtship before finally saying, "Oui, you may have a say". Where Britain handed its dominions parliaments and courts, France and Portugal left chaos, coups, or client strongmen.

These values are not locked in museums, nor carved only in stone. They live in queues at bus stops, in Sunday roasts, in civil arguments over tea or a beer, in the small courtesies of daily life. They live whenever someone says "sorry" when they've been bumped, or when strangers laugh together at the weather. They are fragile, yes, but they are also enduring.

And they worked because Britain was confident. Confident enough to argue without fragmenting, to expand without crushing, to reform without collapsing.

But today Britain is in danger of forgetting who it is. The high-trust society that was Britain has been traded away for the private vanity of an elite wanting to belong to a club, any club, as long as it was not British.

No other nation has done more to advance freedom, fairness, and prosperity. The task now is not to apologise for this record, but to protect it—and to ensure that those who join Britain share in the values that made it what it is. This is not arrogance. It is continuity and common sense. And it is why, of all the nations in history, Britain can truly claim to have led humanity forward.

The Tower of Babel fell when its builders lost their common tongue. Britain's tower will fall if it forgets its values. But it need not. Britain has been here before: divided, self-doubting, weary. And every time, it found a way back. The answer is not despair, but rediscovery. Not apology, but confidence. Not Babel, but Britain.

If this book has reminded you of anything, I hope it is this: that Britain's greatness lies not in empire or wealth, but in the stubborn kindness of its people, in their humour, their fairness, and their refusal to give up.

We live in troubled times. The tower may feel shaky, the voices discordant. But Britain has rebuilt before, and it can do so again—if it remembers who it is.

Britain's Values as a Beacon for the World

The world today is not short of problems. Wars grind on in Europe and the Middle East, while the United Nations mostly issues strongly worded letters. Migration pressures are straining borders from the Mediterranean to the Rio Grande. Debt mountains rise in every advanced economy, kicked forward with promises that "growth will sort it out". Universities once devoted to truth now tremble at the wrong opinions. Tech giants play with artificial intelligence and deepfakes while governments shuffle policy papers marked "too complicated". And in many countries, corruption, cronyism, and populist rage eat away at weak institutions already undermined by their opponents.

Global institutions creak under their own weight. Treaties sprawl into irrelevance. Foreign aid often disappears into bureaucracies and private bank accounts or props up regimes with little interest in liberty. In this fog, Britain's distinct set of values—hammered out over centuries of argument and persistence—offers not just nostalgia, but a way forward.

Take *Fair Play for All*. International bodies from the United Nations to the European Union promise fairness, yet rules are bent, scandals buried, and smaller nations sidelined where more powerful countries are concerned. Britain's tradition of one law for all—whether in Parliament, on the football pitch, or in the courts—is a reminder that fairness must be visible, not just proclaimed.

Or consider *Owning Our Mistakes*. When Britain errs, it holds inquiries, publishes the findings, and recalibrates. Compare that with institutions like the UN Human Rights Council, which often seats authoritarian states busily violating the very rights they are meant to uphold. It's a bit like appointing the local poacher to run the gamekeepers' union. Transparency is the British way, and it is what the world craves in an era of suspicion and disinformation.

Evolution, Not Revolution may be Britain's most exportable gift. Today, as nations wrestle with climate policy, digital disruption, and migration, this value is a guide: slow down, consult, carry people with you, correct course in daylight.

In the end, cultures adapt to circumstances and the values that underpin the culture are created as a result—it's what they do. Cultures bend and twist with history, sometimes flourishing, sometimes floundering. The test is simple enough: do your values make your people safer, healthier, better educated, happier, and more prosperous? If they do, keep them. If they don't, then borrow a page from Britain's playbook. You could do a lot worse. Which is precisely why Britain must rediscover its own values now, before it drifts further into the cul-de-sac of Davos jargon, globalist daydreams, apocalyptic fever dreams and progressive platitudes—all fine words but never tested by fire.

Britain's values, by contrast, have been hammered on the anvil of centuries, and we know—with the certainty of lived proof—that they deliver. To abandon them is not just careless; it risks turning the world's most quietly admired nation into a punchline. And if there's one thing the British cannot abide, it's becoming a laughingstock.

Epilogue: Play Your Part

A guide for Britons and those who've joined them on this damp, but determined, island

Britain's values aren't dusty artefacts in a glass case. They live in the rhythm of the comment about the weather to a stranger, the raised eyebrow at bad behaviour, and the self-deprecating joke when the roof leaks. Your duty is to speak out against ideas which fall outside British values that leaders want to impose on you: ideas that make them seem virtuous to the rest of the world but damage your way of life. To keep your values alive, they must be practised and insisted upon—daily—by Britons and newcomers alike.

For Britons Themselves

Lest you forget your own peculiar genius

The British genius begins in the queue. It isn't simply about waiting your turn—it's civilisation in miniature, where duke and dustman stand side by side, governed by the same invisible rules. Fair play continues in the way you speak: everyone has the right to grumble about the Prime Minister, the weather, the latest globalist or Davos idea, non-British behaviour or the price of pints. Suspicion of power is a national sport, whether in Fleet Street cartoons or muttered jokes about quangos or pie-in-the-sky ideologies which promise everything and deliver misery.

Joining in means bringing a sponge cake to the fête, buying a raffle ticket, or clapping politely even when the amateur dramatics are dreadful. Mistakes? Continue to own them—sometimes with a full inquiry, sometimes with a sheepish apology, but never with silence. *Duty before self* hums in the background.

And when life turns grim, keep reaching for humour before despair: the banana that goes from green to rotten in one day, the bus that never comes. Britain changes slowly. Incremental reforms are maddening, but they've saved you from chasing the gold at the end of the rainbow which is never there. Yet this patience doesn't mean stasis. Continue to push boundaries: in science, art, music, finance, business and sometimes even politics.

Don't be tempted to be fashionable or virtuous by rewriting your great past as if shame were the only lens. Your genius lies in correcting, not erasing. Insist that the full story be told. Finally, don't let comedians be the only ones to critique society. You are all court jesters at heart.

For Non-Britons

A survival guide to thriving, not just surviving

Do not arrive in Britain expecting a guilt-fuelled banquet where the locals pay and you merely eat. This island is not a welfare cornucopia for those unwilling to join in, nor is it a blank slate on which to project the values of the country you chose to leave. Criticising Britain while living apart from it, clutching the customs of elsewhere while demanding the privileges of here, is not integration—it is parasitism. And parasitism breeds resentment faster than British rain ruins a picnic.

Britain does not ask you to erase your past, only to respect its present. Play your part, contribute more than you receive, and you will be embraced. Treat it as a debtor nation owing you tribute, and you'll find the welcome mat quietly rolled up beneath your feet. And don't blame the British when this happens.

Those who join Britain soon discover that the country is stitched together by subtle rituals that need to be observed and learnt. Being offered a cup of tea is less a drink than a peace treaty; the two-minute silence is a national heartbeat; the weather joke is the universal password.

Respect the invisible bubble —an arm's length is not coldness, but dignity. See the rules as solidarity: "Keep off the grass" is less about the lawn and more about playing fair. Behave politely and respectfully in the public square. Don't play your music on the bus as if civilisation needs your playlist, or mistake tolerance for support.

Smile, say hello, share a joke and help. Adopting British values is not betraying your culture but showing respect to the one in which you now find yourself living. Belonging is made of nods, smiling with your mouth as well as your eyes, and quiet kindnesses, not emotional outbursts.

Learn to laugh at yourself *before* others do—nothing wins affection faster. Integration is not about government manifestos but about small gestures: standing respectfully on Remembrance Day, or helping an old lady with her shopping bag.

Respect Britain's monuments: they are not yours and you may dislike them in a culture that is not British, but they are theirs. They may signify something very different to what you think you see.

Join in the British Way—get involved in bettering the life of the British people, not your community. Your community's life will be bettered as a result.

Britain also speaks a coded language. "That's interesting" really means "please stop". "I don't think so" means "not until hell freezes over". And "Go on then" usually means "I'd love to". Cracking these understatement codes is vital, as I found out in my first year.

In many countries, being loud (talking at high volume, laughing boisterously, calling across the room) is taken as a sign of warmth, enthusiasm, or welcome. But in Britain, that same behaviour often comes across as utterly appalling. It is seen as intrusive or inconsiderate, not endearing. Shouting across the Tube, blasting music on your phone, or talking on speaker in public is not "colourful"; it's theft of everyone else's peace. You may think you're radiating sunshine, but to British ears you're setting off the car alarm.

Don't roam the market square in gangs as if occupying the territory. You will be noticed far more for helping an old person across the street, or for holding the door open, than for marching or hanging out together.

Don't overshare your emotional life in public. No one is interested in the details, and the British are allergic to such earnestness.

Don't take British criticism of themselves to each other as actual criticism. If you agree too eagerly that Britain is falling apart, you'll meet the bulldog spirit under the jacket.

Don't confuse politeness with weakness. The nation that produced Magna Carta, the Spitfire, and the NHS has limits.

Think what you can do for Britain and the Britons, not what they and Britain can do for you.

Bibliography

This book doesn't use footnotes or academic references. Instead, here's a curated list of works—history, politics, culture, polemic—works that illuminate Britain's values, achievements, and dilemmas. They reflect a wide spectrum of perspectives: from the celebratory to the sceptical, from the conservative to the progressive. Together, they give a richer picture of the conversation in which this book plays its part.

Further Reading

Akala, Natives: *Race and Class in the Ruins of Empire* (Two Roads, 2019).

Bennett, Sam, *Constructions of Migrant Integration in British Public Discourse: Becoming British* (Palgrave Macmillan, 2019).

Cannadine, Sir David, *Ornamentalism: How the British Saw Their Empire* (Oxford University Press, 2001).

Colley, Linda, *Britons: Forging the Nation 1707–1837* (Yale University Press, 1992).

Fryer, Peter, *Staying Power: The History of Black People in Britain* (Pluto Press, 1984; reissued 2010).

Gilroy, Paul, *There Ain't No Black in the Union Jack: The Cultural Politics of Race and Nation* (Hutchinson, 1987).

Goodwin, Matthew, *Values, Voice and Virtue: The New British Politics* (Penguin, 2023).

Hatherley, Owen, *The Alienation Effect: Émigré Lives and Postwar Culture in Britain* (Verso, 2025).

Hitchens, Peter, *The Abolition of Britain: From Lady Chatterley to Tony Blair* (Quartet Books, 2000).

Hoque, Aminul, *British-Islamic Identity: Third-generation Bangladeshis from East London* (Trentham Books, 2015).

Keane, John, *The Life and Death of Democracy* (Simon & Schuster, 2009).

Morlino, Leonardo and Gianluigi Palombella (eds.), *Rule of Law and Democracy: Inquiries into Internal and External Issues* (Brill, 2010).

Mount, Ferdinand, *Soft: A Brief History of Sentimentality* (Bloomsbury Continuum, 2025).

Parekh, Bhikhu, *Rethinking Multiculturalism: Cultural Diversity and Political Theory* (Palgrave Macmillan, 2002).

Phillips, Melanie, *All Must Have Prizes* (Little, Brown, 1996).

Phillips, Melanie, *The World Turned Upside Down* (Encounter Books, 2010).

Selwood, Dominic, *Anatomy of a Nation: A History of British Identity in 50 Documents* (Constable, 2021).

Shukla, Nikesh (ed.), *The Good Immigrant* (Unbound, 2016).

Sidwell, Marc, *The Long March: How the Left Won the Culture War and What to Do About It* (New Culture Forum, 2020).

Starkey, David, *Crown and Country: A History of England through the Monarchy* (Harper Press, 2010).

Sumption, Jonathan, *The Challenges of Democracy: And the Rule of Law* (Profile Books, 2025).

About the Author

Gavin Fraser was born in George, South Africa, in 1958. He completed school a year ahead of schedule and, at 17, spent a year in Nova Scotia, Canada, as a Rotary Exchange Student. Returning to South Africa, he earned a degree in Chemical Engineering at the University of Cape Town, spending his holidays working at a mine. He then completed his mandatory military service as an officer in the South African Navy.

After the Navy, Gavin joined an international oil company in Cape Town, rising quickly to a senior position. By day he worked in business; by night he sang in the chorus of the local opera house while simultaneously studying part-time for both an MBA and a Bachelor of Musicology.

In 1988 he moved to Johannesburg to join an international management consultancy linked to one of the "top six" accounting firms of the era, specialising in business strategy and corporate culture analysis and change. Three years later, in 1991, he was offered a position in London with a consultancy applying emerging management theories from business schools such as Harvard and INSEAD. He was seconded to work directly with two leading professors and specialised in rapid mass transformation of businesses in trouble. In 1998 he became a partner at Andersen Consulting (now Accenture), where he remained until their IPO in 2001. Afterward, he took a short sabbatical to record two singer-songwriter albums, which he released 15 years later, and enjoyed landscaping seven gardens.

Gavin then founded his own consultancy, specialising in strategy, innovation, and leadership transformation. Over the next two decades he worked in more than 35 countries across every continent. Alongside his business career, he pursued his passion for music: recording Mozart's Symphonies Nos. 40 and 41 with the Danube Symphony Orchestra in Budapest. These recordings became chart-topping interpretations of two of the most frequently recorded works in the classical music repertoire and remain among the most streamed recordings today.

He now divides his time between writing music, researching and writing books, landscaping gardens, and travelling. His first book, *The Moral Stress of Nations* (2020), explored how behavioural genetics and Jonathan Haidt's Moral Foundations Theory suggest that political leanings may be innate, genetically determined. He sets out to prove that coalition governments which evolve gradually and remain anchored in the free, rather than authoritarian centre, create the happiest nations.

Gavin is based between the UK, Europe, and Asia, and has three children.

Printed in Dunstable, United Kingdom

73604797R00068